THE
CURTAIN

- A NOVEL -

PATRICK ORD

DEDICATION

To my family . . . and families everywhere.

ACKNOWLEDGMENTS

To my wife Emily who encouraged me to put my thoughts on paper, was understanding enough to be without the help of her husband while I worked countless hours on this manuscript, and who had the faith that my efforts would ultimately be of worth.

To my children who reflect the best within me. This novel is a modest attempt of trying to make the world a better place for you.

To my mother and father who read countless drafts and found value in my early efforts when I sometimes saw none. To my four brothers: Jonathan, Andrew, Michael, and Peter for always having my back and for being outstanding brothers, husbands, and fathers.

To Steve for being the inspiration behind Henry Maddox and providing me with the technical and marketing concepts that drove the story.

To Tyler Smith at *Liberty Springs* for his encouragement and in helping me understand the science and concerns related to process addictions.

To Greg Hammond for reading the first forty pages of an extremely rough draft and making early suggestions – many of which survived the final edits.

And finally to Dave King, my editor, who saw what I was trying to do and made it better.

PROLOGUE

He stopped in the middle of the bridge, just where the suspension lines dipped. Nothing obstructed the view to the east and west. He bailed out of the car, hopped over the rail onto the pedestrian walkway on the east side of the bridge, and began to scramble up onto the cable itself. Behind him traffic piled up as other passengers started to gather around him.

The forty mile an hour winds caused the entire bridge to sway slightly. He stumbled crossing the cable walkway but held himself steady at the bridge's outer railing.

"We have a jumper!" A woman pointed at him.

"Give him space," someone yelled.

"Don't do it!"

"Life gets better."

The crowd grew larger. They began to close in on him.

He scanned their faces. Hundreds of people were now looking at him, fearful for his safety, hungry for the excitement. He was the center of attention.

Showtime.

"I guess you didn't expect this, did you?" he yelled. "But then again, this makes your jobs much easier, doesn't it? Why get your hands messy, when I can do the dirty work myself? Sound familiar? Do you suppose distancing yourself from the dirt keeps your hands clean? We're all guilty!"

He swung his legs over the outer railing and hung on with one hand. Nothing now separated him from the sea below.

The bridge was now a parking lot. Law enforcement began to break through the crowd, moving toward him.

"Take out your cell phone cameras," he said.

The wind carried away his command.

"Take out your cameras," he shouted. "Or I *will* jump."

People looked down, most of them anyway.

"Don't pretend to be ashamed! We're a culture of opportunists, eager to make our mark through YouTube or the evening news. Why should it make you uncomfortable to actually see the face of your victim? Take out your cameras!"

"He said take out your cameras people," a lady yelled, "now!"

One by one, cell phones appeared.

"Now record!" he said. "Believe me, you won't want to miss this."

For the love of money
is the root of all evil…

- 1 Timothy 6:10 (KJV)

CHAPTER 1

16 months earlier

The room was dark, except for the images projected onto the screen. Copious amounts of data synthesized and presented in the form of charts, matrices, and bullet points. The slides served the dual purpose of informing the audience and illuminating the presenter.

Professor Henry Maddox pressed the remote to bring up the next chart, changing the hue of the room from a disquieting orange to a more subliminally friendly blue. "The Video Gaming Industry has been estimated to be worth up to $65 Billion," Henry said, "which is about the size of the entire global music industry and worldwide movie industry – combined. Yet Zynthe Gaming represents a mere fraction of this market – less than 1 percent as of last quarter. Strategies that have been used successfully in other forms of media to entice consumers are yet in their infancy within the gaming industry. If you were to implement these strategies before your competitors, you could multiply your revenues tenfold within one year. I've given you the data. You tell me, where are your opportunities?"

The ten executives huddled around the small conference room table, each waiting for someone else to make the first comment. Gerald Burke, Zynthe's CEO, had summoned them with an "all hands on deck" text message late the night before. The meeting had been billed as a strategy session. The urgency of the request suggested something critical, desperate.

It was the way Henry wanted it. He often found that people were more creative if you pushed them off center.

"I didn't pay top dollar to hire all of you MBAs to sit there and *look* smart," Burke said. "I want some answers."

"Well, based on the 2010 Entertainment Software Rating Board data, 49 percent of all gamers fall within the range of 18 to 49 years old." The respondent was Chief Product Officer, David Yeo, a slight man with a surfer's build. Henry had actually been expecting to hear from their vice-president of marketing, Blair Johns, first, but it looked like Johns was still processing the information. He'd take Yeo for now.

"The average age of a gamer is 34 years old," Yeo said. "And 48 percent of games sold are rated 'E' for everyone. It would seem that we should follow the market and target these consumers."

"You seem like an intelligent young man as well as a good note taker," Henry said "I bet you got great grades in graduate school. Your answer couldn't be considered incorrect. Your professor would have no room to argue with your analysis. But we're not in school anymore, are we? Safe answers don't disrupt industries, attract capital, and make people rich."

Henry powered down the projector and turned on the lights.

"If you're intent on following the industry, focusing entirely on seeking out likely gamers, your company will be extinct in a couple of years, and everyone in this room will be unemployed with a tarnished resume. Is that what you want? Is that why I'm here?" Henry shrugged. "Okay, try again."

Henry waited, watching the assembled executives try to avoid the mistake of David Yeo. It was safer to remain silent.

A minute passed.

"Okay, I'll give it a shot." This time it was Blair Johns. "If we look at the trends, fewer people are purchasing video games, and the platforms are moving away from traditional gaming consoles and toward mobile devices like tablets and smart phones. The new games also rely heavily on social networks. The next generation of gaming follows a different revenue model. Users can access games for free, but the games are monetized through micro-transactions."

"Go on." Henry removed his Gucci, Jacquard stitched, suit coat; simultaneously dismissing and calling attention to it. The action claimed status while signaling that he was at one with the people in the room. It was an approach Henry used for rewarding someone for giving a good answer. "Tell us about micro-transactions."

"A micro-transaction would be buying new clothes for an avatar type character, or purchasing currency that could be used in a new digital world. Research has shown that once a gamer is exposed to some of these 'freemium' games, the propensity to upgrade is significant."

"Now you're on the right track my friend," Henry said. "You see, we study data not because we want to perpetuate the status quo but because we want to identify trends."

The other executives nodded at Blair. Gestures intended to thank him from sparing them from further embarrassment.

"Now the next step in the process," Henry said, "is to leverage the emerging trends into a distinct and untapped market. Allow me to present a possible strategic direction for one of your new games."

Henry began to draw a diagram on the white board. He hadn't seen a white board in a corporate conference room in years, but his skills hadn't deserted him. Stick figures, shapes, and connected lines began to clothe Henry's words with imagery.

"As you mentioned," Henry said, "you give away the game for free. You then use social networking to promote your game. Friends will invite other friends to participate – as every marketer knows, the most persuasive advertisement for a product is an endorsement from a friend. Peer pressure will cause users to upgrade. If you're lucky, the game will achieve the holy grail of video gaming . . . it will become viral."

Henry turned back to face the executives and took a step towards them, forcing them to focus. Everyone was now silent, curious.

"And now, the critical point. The purpose of the game is not to persuade the user to invest more heavily into the game world. The purpose is to get the user to provide us with massive quantities of personal information. Give gaming credits when the users tell us their age, their gender, the number of people in their family, the ages of their children, the products they've purchased, the entertainment they consume, where they live, their religion, their favorite movie star – we want to know everything!

"In the end user licensing agreement, which nobody reads, we'll tell the user that by playing our game, they have given us the right to access information relating to other people within their social network. The unsuspecting user will thus not only provide us with their personal data profiles, they'll allow us access to all of their friends' personal data as well."

Henry moved back on the whiteboard, when Richard Moldt, the Chief Technical Officer, interrupted.

"Pardon me Dr. Maddox but don't we need to worry about privacy concerns? How can the video gaming industry extract and exploit someone's personal information with such impunity, while other industries get sued over the same practice? I get all sorts of disclosures from my health insurance company that go to great lengths to convince me that my personal information is safe in their hands."

Henry felt the room drift in Moldt's direction. Not a problem. They'd be even more his when he won them back.

"Welcome to the wonderful world of social networking my friend," he said. "Users on social networks could care less about privacy. Oh sure, every now and again you hear some kickback from a user group griping about Big Brother. The social network inevitably responds with instructions on how to 'opt out' or how to 'reconfigure user preferences.' Few if any users ever bother to learn how to lock down their personal information. As long as the use of the information isn't obviously intrusive, most users will live with the invasion of privacy. Besides, most of those who opt out will return as soon as they realize that in today's culture no social network equals no social life."

"Still," Moldt said, "the whole concept seems really sneaky to me. Wouldn't it be better in the long run to create a compelling user experience rather than exploit a user's personal information for profit?"

"Are you creating a compelling user experience now?"

"We like to think so, yes."

Henry opened his arms and looked around the room, inviting the executives to view their surroundings. Flickering fluorescent bulbs cast intermittent shadows on the aged, oak, conference room table. Periodic squeals of rotating chairs briefly masked the sound of the chairs' grinding wheels against the worn carpet. "How's that working out for you?"

Moldt looked chastened. Now was the time to reel him back in.

"Listen, you're free to follow that course if you wish," Henry said. "*My* moral imperative is to show you the future. When I run into you at a coffee shop in a couple of years, I want you to tell me about the big house on the hill you just bought. I want you to tell me about the great schools your kids are attending. I want you to be better off for having taken my advice. Why do you think social networking sites are so valuable? You can't be so naïve to think the service they offer alone merits such values do you? The worth of social networks is in their data. This data can be sold, it can be used to court marketers, it can be monetized in so many different ways that we haven't yet even begun to imagine. Sure, people won't want their health history shared with the public. But if you're using their information to steer them toward goods and services that they're interested in, they'll actually thank you for that."

They still weren't entirely with him. No worries. Everyone brought up the conventional ethical concerns, at first. Those concerns were appropriate for little, street-corner businesses. He had to show them that they didn't fit the modern world.

"Research has shown that video games are among the most effective ways of extracting personal information from a user," he said. "Role playing games are the best because people feel much freer to reveal the most intimate of personal preferences – data they would never reveal to even their best friend – when they're creating an online alter-ego. We can use this information to allow retailers to better target customers."

"But does the customer or any of us really understand all of the other ways this personal information might be used?" Moldt asked. "Shouldn't we at least provide a privacy protection notice and allow them to opt out of certain types of information sharing?"

Henry gave him his best patient smile. "Sure. Put it in the user agreement. My point is that it won't matter. Most social network users won't care. If they really cared about their privacy, they wouldn't be on a social network in the first place. Pandora's information sharing box has been opened. Your only decision now is whether you or someone else will profit off of the data."

"Enough discussion for today," CEO Gerald Burke said. "Let's give Professor Maddox a hand for his presentation."

Henry deferred to the CEO. He'd missed Burke's discomfort with the way things were going. Given another ten minutes, he'd have been able to win the room over. But it didn't matter. He'd bring them around in the end, starting with Burke.

Over the polite applause, Burke motioned to Henry. "Henry, I would like to have a word with you in private."

The executives gathered their belongings and scurried out of the conference room. Henry moved to the end of the table to sit by Burke.

"Henry," he said, "I know you're right, but I can't chart this course for the company unless I can sell the vision internally. I think there's too much resistance."

"Don't worry about the kickback," Henry said. "I have a solution for that."

"Which is?"

"Buy each of your executives a car."

"What? Henry, we need to tighten our belts, not go on a spending spree."

"No. You can't afford to waste money at this point, but this will be the best money you'll ever spend."

Gerald nodded. "Okay, I'll bite. Keep going."

"Increase each executive's compensation by including a car allowance. Establish relationships with each of the major luxury car retailers in the area. With this new car allowance, each executive will now be able to qualify for a loan to purchase their new luxury automobile. Put each executive's loan in their name, not the company's. This way if an executive wants to leave the company, the car payments then becomes his or her personal obligation."

"All right, that gives them an incentive to stay."

"More than that. Get the executives excited. Make an event out of it. Have every executive drive their new car to a corporate retreat. Make them feel like a million bucks. Tell them you want people to notice them, to build buzz here in the valley. Show everyone that all of the Zynthe Gaming executives are doing well. This will, in fact, attract some attention from investor types."

"Okay, so I write a bunch of checks to get the attention of people who write bigger checks. How is this going to help my business?"

"I only scratched the surface of my recommended gaming strategy. You're going to need a greater commitment from each one of your executives to implement the whole vision. The cars are a start."

"You're not going to advise that I do something illegal are you?"

"There is never long-term profit in doing anything illegal. It gets too complicated, too quickly, and you do tend to lose the best and brightest. But you should know that no one gets ahead unless they're willing to push the envelope."

"Go on."

"The success of your business depends on keeping users within your gaming experience for as long as possible. When they leave, you need to be able to draw them back in. In other words, you need to addict your users, literally."

"What do you mean, literally?"

"Recent science confirms that process addictions are often times more compelling than chemical addictions."

"What does that mean?"

"Chemical addictions result from consuming some sort of substance – alcohol, drugs. Process addictions result from a routine or behavior that stimulates the limbic system of the brain to the point that the brain floods the body with dopamine. The dopamine provides a high, just like a chemical addiction, so the user therefore wants to revisit the behavior again and again. The addiction occurs when the rational part of the brain – the frontal cortex – is overrun by the emotional part of the brain – the limbic system. The user gets to the point that he craves the dopamine producing behaviors more than family, friendship, sleep, and even food."

"So how do we addict users to a video game?"

"You're already doing it. The experience of overcoming obstacles and winning the game provides your customers with that addictive rush – that's the point of what you do. You merely want to provide targeted rewards for certain behaviors within the game. The trick is – and this is the key – you want to increase the intensity and frequency of these online rewards over time. This will increase the dopamine reward the user experiences and intensify the addiction."

Burke looked down at his notes and then back at Henry. "Henry, I don't know if I feel comfortable making money off of a bunch of zombies plugged into my games. Certainly, this strategy will become public and we would get shut down."

"No, Gerald, you're not getting it. As a gaming company, you already take the user to a certain threshold of addiction. I'm talking about doing what you already do, but doing it better. This will be no different than people that get addicted to chocolate or exercise. Then, all you need to do is provide a gateway to other, more addictive stimuli."

"And how would I do that?"

"Do you recall when I started to describe the vision for Zynthe that I mentioned users would have the opportunity to accrue gaming credits by answering questions about themselves? I also want credits to be earned when the users provide information about their friends and family. So if the user provides her friend's name, dress size, and favorite clothing brand, for example, the user will get credits, and the friend will get online ads targeted to their preferences. The friend will also be invited to participate in the game and earn credits as well. This encourages the whole viral notion of the game."

"I'm with you, but I haven't heard anything jaw dropping yet."

"The value of your gaming credits will depend on the exchange rate. We'll of course do the usual things like partner with retailers for discounts and purchases – still minor addictions. Where we push the envelope, however, is that we'll allow a method of exchange to access online gambling and pornography sites. This is where the addictions really take hold."

"We become a gateway to addict our users to these types of sites?"

"Exactly. Your credits will allow the users access to these sites only on a trial basis, however. After that, the user has to pay. You can structure a deal with these more addictive sites where you can get a recurring commission for every dollar your user spends. These types of businesses do this all the time. They know that, once they get the customers, they seldom lose them. They are therefore willing to pay generously to acquire customers. This will provide a continuous stream of revenue for Zynthe."

"Okay, I like the money potential, but I'm still uneasy about getting into the gambling and pornography business."

"That is the beauty of this model. You won't. You just direct people in those directions and profit off of them. These revenues will show up on your income statement as 'partner commissions,' and that's exactly what they'll be. And as far as I can see, directing someone to a pornography or gambling site they would enjoy is no more morally problematic than directing them to a shopping site they would enjoy."

"But what if some of our underage users access some of this adult content? Do we have any liability there?"

"Absolutely not. Each of these adult websites is in charge of making sure they have the appropriate controls in place to keep underage users away. You're merely a referral site. And if you'd like additional legal protection, you can issue a disclaimer notice whenever the user accesses any of your partner sites. You'll tell the user that they're leaving your site and that Zynthe can't be held responsible for anything that occurs on the referred site."

"Well this all is certainly making more sense. Now if I can only get all of my other executives on board."

"Don't tell your executives about this new wrinkle until after the site is tested and launched – and after they've had their new cars for about six months. At that point, they'll be so used to the feel of their leather seats they won't give your partner agreements a second thought."

"So regarding your fee –"

"Gerald, for this type of deal, I don't want any upfront money. I don't even want a percentage of sales."

"So, what do you get out of it?"

"All I want is your data."

Even while we sleep
We will find you
Acting on your best behavior
Turn your back on Mother Nature
Everybody wants to rule the world

- Tears For Fears,
"Everybody Wants To Rule The World" (1985)

CHAPTER 2

Henry let himself out of the industrial-park warehouse that housed Zynthe Gaming offices and entered the parking lot. He pulled his iPhone from his jacket pocket, checked for bars, and tweeted the following:

> Just left the offices of Zynthe Gaming. Discussed new strategy. Zynthe will b hottest gaming co. in valley.

Henry had a Twitter following of only about 22,000 – relatively modest, but they made up for it in clout. Henry's followers included top venture capitalists, investment bankers, Wall Street analysts, and hedge fund managers. Early stage investors had dumped money into new ventures based on his endorsement alone, and his twitter feeds on occasion even moved the stock price of major companies. Such was the power of social networking technology combined with a reputation for picking winners. He had been approached multiple times by businesses wanting to pay him to tweet something noteworthy about their products or services. He rarely turned down money, but he had to maintain a strict integrity with his tweets. He would only endorse a business if they were his client and only if they committed to following his advice. That was his brand, and he needed to protect it.

Zynthe Gaming was struggling to convince the investment market they were worthy of second round financing. Up to this point, they had not met their growth goals. Henry's tweet alone would change that.

Burke's call to Henry came a day prior and in a panic. There was a little bit of risk in throwing all in with Zynthe up front – Burke was clearly wary of ceding so much control to Henry – but Henry was confident he would come around. And the calls Burke would be getting from venture capitalists for the rest of the morning would cement the relationship.

Zynthe was now part of Henry's data analytics empire. Henry took great pride in identifying trends. He took stock as compensation during the dot com boom and cashed out before the inevitable crash. He even bet against the real estate market via credit default swaps and won big as others suffered. Having already amassed more cash than he could spend in a lifetime, Henry could now move to a different method of payment. Henry's new compensation was not so much about wealth. He now wanted control.

Technology had created an interconnected world. People could now leverage their personal networks in ways that were previously impossible. Few understood the opportunity in manipulating these networks. Henry had studied the informatics. He knew that the next big thing was data collection and analysis. A data land grab was underway and the winner would emerge with unprecedented influence.

Henry arrived at his East Bay office within ninety minutes. The office was located by the Berkeley campus. It was originally a dilapidated, single story, mid-century ranch house. He had restored the home to its Leave it to Beaver glory and repurposed it to his office. He liked the intimate, understated feel of the architecture – no imposing mahogany reception area, an actual working kitchen. He figured that since he spent more time at the office than at his home, he would make his office feel like a home. High-end visitors were sometimes unimpressed. But he seldom had visitors and after meeting with clients, he needed a sanctuary, not a stage.

His only employee was Cheryl Goodwin, his office manager, scheduler, bookkeeper, and general go to. Cheryl was thirty-two years old and single, the only child to a single mother. Though most of Cheryl's High School classmates struggled to advance; thanks to a relentless mother and a collegiate track scholarship, Cheryl had not only made it to college, she had graduated with honors.

Cheryl wasn't opposed to getting married, but it wasn't a priority either. She certainly didn't want to replay her mother's single parent lifestyle, though she and her mother were still very close. So although Cheryl had plenty of attention from aspiring suitors, none had been able to meet her uncompromising standards. Her loyalty now was only to those who had earned her trust – her mother and Henry.

Over the ten years he had employed her, Henry had learned to return that trust. Cheryl had been with Henry since he was only a full time professor who wanted to find a way to better monetize his research. At first, he'd thought their working relationship might blossom into something more – Cheryl was a knockout. But her no nonsense attitude quashed any of Henry's romantic advances, and he was glad in the end. Their working relationship was much more valuable than any quick hook-up ever could have been. He hired out most of his data mining and IT functions and trusted the people he worked with. But in most important aspects, he and Cheryl were the heart of the firm. That's why, in a moment of honesty five years earlier, he had given her a 10 percent stake in the company, now worth millions.

"What happened with Zynthe this morning?" Cheryl asked as he dropped his laptop bag under the coat rack near the door.

"If they take my advice, within six months Zynthe will be the hottest company in one of the fastest growing industries on the planet."

"Good to know. How should I bill them?"

"No fee. I got their data instead."

Cheryl raised an eyebrow. "I'm told that most successful businesses charge actual money for what they do."

"Cheryl, once we have our client's data, the money will come. Be patient. Have I ever misled you?"

Henry grabbed a bottle of sparkling water from a restored enameled Coke machine behind the reception. He dropped into one of the nearby Nixon Leather Chairs, draped one leg over the armrest, and took a swig.

"A lot of companies that you think are making money on their operations are actually in the business of collecting data. Social networks for example are really data collection companies. The gaming industry is moving to this model very quickly as well. The video gaming experience has become a tool to extract personal data from the user. *People* are these businesses' products. The whole digital experience is just a gimmick to draw them in. This was why I met with Zynthe today."

Cheryl stopped her filing, walked around the reception desk and took a seat across from Henry. "What about dating sites?"

"Now you're thinking. Yes, they have massive amounts of personal data and yes they use the data to make money."

"Isn't this kind of scary though? I can only imagine what they have on me. Isn't this data secured by their privacy policy?"

"Oh, yeah, they won't resell your personal data, not in most cases. That doesn't mean your data isn't valuable to them or others, though. A dating website for example may commit not to disclose your individual data – name, address, e-mail – to outside companies, but their privacy policy probably allows that your data may be aggregated and used or sold as part of a larger sample set."

"Why would I care about an anonymous aggregate of my data?"

"No reason at all. But if I can access aggregate data, I can identify trends. I can tell which user profiles get the most hits for instance."

"That's easy though, it's always the most attractive people."

Henry adjusted his posture to where he was now leaning forward with his forearms on his legs. His shoulders were squared and directed towards Cheryl. "But what do people consider attractive? The data for example may show that dating profiles with the most hits have a profile picture of a blonde girl from twenty five to thirty years-old – not so surprising. On further analysis, however, we may find that the majority of these profile pictures have the women looking to their left. Now I don't know what this would mean, but I don't need to know what it means in order to profit from it. The data could also suggest that people who use the word 'active' in their profile get more hits than those that don't. Perhaps, profiles with certain ethnicities and of certain religious backgrounds get more interest as well. The point is that after exhaustive data analysis, we can create the perfect dating profile that is assured to get the most amounts of hits."

"This is all fine and good Henry but what does it matter if the person isn't real?"

"What if I'm selling a product? Using the aggregate data of a dating website, I could go find a pitch person with the most universally attractive attributes. Wouldn't that sell more products? In print ads, I wouldn't even need a real person since I could digitally enhance the photograph to exactly match the ideal."

"So you can create more effective marketing campaigns?"

"That's one of the attractions." Henry finished his sparkling water and tossed the empty bottle across the room and towards a trash can. The bottle careened off the rim and fell on the floor. He grimaced.

"Don't underestimate the value of marketing, Cheryl. What if we had enough data to create the perfect Presidential candidate? Couldn't we then go out and find someone who matched the profile and then indoctrinate them with the positions that could win an election? This is already happening today with speech analysis – firms exist that tell candidates the most effective way to phrase certain issues to garner the most support. Candidates will talk about how they're against the 'death tax' as opposed to the 'inheritance tax' or how they are for the 'war on terror' as opposed to 'the war in Iraq.' These decisions are all based on data. Don't forget that our politicians are nothing more than sales people for certain causes. The causes with the most effective sales people always win."

"So the people that have the data will have the power to influence our lives."

"They can sell the data off to the highest bidder, keep the data and provide strategic advice to companies or causes, or manipulate masses of people into doing what *they* want. *They* will be able to control culture. Currently, I'm content to provide the strategic advice. I don't really want to rule the world . . . yet."

"What a world it would be if you were ruling it Henry. I can't begin to imagine."

"And that's the point Cheryl. This data is too important to trust with just anyone. That's why it's so valuable. And that's why I want it." Henry got out of his chair, scooped his empty water bottle off the ground, and tossed it in the trash. "Do you remember that telematics company that I consulted with about a year ago?" Henry asked.

"Yeah, Onboard."

"Right."

"And what did they do again?"

"They used global positioning satellite technology to contact emergency personnel if you got in a car accident. They could provide you with audible directions to your destination. They could even open your car door or start your car if you lost your keys. Most all auto manufacturers are now offering OnBoard types of services for their vehicles.

"I convinced them to not only track the location of the vehicles but to also track customer driving patterns."

"Driving patterns?"

"How many miles do they drive in a day? Do they wear their seatbelts? How fast do they drive? Oh, and I also had them insert language in their privacy policies so that they could track the data for not only subscribers but for anyone who had the OnBoard technology installed in their car."

"So, thousands of people don't know their driving behavior is being monitored?"

"More like millions, but yeah."

"And what are you doing with all of that data?"

"Right now, we're just archiving it. Eventually, though, we could sell it to insurance companies who want to know how safe a given driver is. We could partner with law enforcement agencies. We could even sell it to marketing firms who then could customize advertising based on your physical location."

"Like air an ad for a coffee shop as you drive past it?"

"Or better yet, offer a promotion to buy coffee at a shop that is in a certain range of your vehicle and have your discount increase as you get closer to the store. You could also create a time component where the promotion expires within a number of minutes. In sales, you always want to combine a promotion with an expiration to create urgency. Of course we would advertise the exact type of coffee you liked to drink as well, which we would know from the coffee vendor's loyalty card program."

Cheryl pulled her braided hair back into a loose pony tail. Several stray strands fell to the sides of her face, settling against her deep, brown skin. Henry fought to maintain focus.

"Essentially we're going from consumers watching advertisements to advertisements watching the consumer," he said as he recovered his train of thought.

"So how much information have we collected?" Cheryl asked.

"Well, we have strategic data sharing agreements with about thirty different companies thus far, and we're pretty well represented in all the major industries. All of our agreements allow us to sell or use the data as we see fit . . . as long as it's legal."

"Don't you worry about laws being passed that would make it illegal to use this type of data?"

"Every major company on the planet has a vested interest in this data collection. There's no way they'd outlaw it."

"So what can consumers do?"

"Why should they do anything? All of this is aimed at giving people more of what they want. Last I checked, that was a good thing. And if we can make a profit at it, so much the better."

There's nothing
on it worthwhile,
and we're not going to watch it
in this household,
and I don't want it
in your intellectual diet.

- Philo T. Farnsworth
(the inventor of the television) to his son

CHAPTER 3

One Week Later

It was February, the worst time of year to visit New York City. Although January was colder, the excitement of the New Year seemed to linger and moderate the chill. March offered the hope of warmth, and November and December brought with them parades and levity. February had nothing. There was Valentine's Day of course, a holiday that Henry detested – a man who couldn't sustain a romantic relationship for more than six months wasn't open to celebrating commitment.

Henry's plane had touched down around five o'clock in the afternoon. He had just enough time to check into his hotel, get cleaned up, and get to the restaurant for the eight o'clock reservation with Melvin.

Melvin Entz's media empire began in London with a single publication in January of 1965 called *Rumour Millrag*. The British magazine was an instant success. Readers feasted on the candid photos of prominent people in compromising situations with provocative, largely invented, headlines. The stories were structured in a way that the unfounded gossip could never be disproved, and readers never really cared that it couldn't be proven, either.

Melvin decided he would sell the magazine at cost and make his money on advertising. He calculated that if he could produce content that would attract gullible readers, these same people would also be indiscriminate consumers. The advertising spots attracted charlatans who sold useless products to stupid people, and *Rumour Millrag* moved mounds of merchandise.

Within a year, Melvin Entz was a millionaire. He used the *Rumour Millrag* business model to develop similar magazines in other markets under separate names. Within ten years, Melvin had gone to daily distribution in over twenty separate countries.

In 1976, Melvin Entz established Entz Media. He also became a U.S. citizen. He bought movie theater chains, a movie production studio, record labels, and radio stations. In the 1980s, Entz media started their own cable television news channel as well as a cable movie subscription channel. He developed amusement parks and created television channels targeting children. Entz's holdings extended into international media markets, where they owned foreign television stations and news channels. With the advent of the internet in the nineties, Entz Media gobbled up online properties. By 2006 Entz owned the top social media sites and over a dozen video gaming companies.

Entz had become the third largest media conglomerate in the world. Over the past ten years, Entz Media had also been Henry's largest client. Henry had kept Entz current on evolving marketing strategies, and Entz Media had made a lot of money in the process. Now Henry had a new direction to discuss with Melvin.

Henry arrived at Entz Media's midtown headquarters overlooking Central Park at 7:45 pm. The Entz Media Center was two, eighty story buildings connected by one pedestrian bridge at the fiftieth floor. The top floor of the South East tower housed a ten thousand square foot penthouse that Melvin Entz used for one of his state side residences. A Japanese restaurant, "Shibui", that was considered to be one of the finest dining experiences in Manhattan, was located on the top floor of the other tower. The restaurant only sat thirty people. All reservations had to be approved by Mr. Entz himself.

Henry approached the North West tower through the side entrance, which landed him at the building's security station.

"Mr. Maddox, it's a pleasure to see you sir," said a barrel-chested security guard dressed in a black suit, white shirt, and black tie. "I understand that you're here to dine with Mr. Entz at Shibui."

Henry nodded.

"Please follow me to the express elevator." The man walked through a labyrinth of hallways while flashing a security fob that unlocked various doors along the way. Once in the elevator, the man again swiped his fob. The elevator doors closed and then accelerated to the eightieth floor.

"Shibui will be down the hall to the left."

Henry stopped at Shibui and then deliberately went past it. He had arrived early and wanted to use the extra time to explore the rooftop. As he continued to the end of the hallway, an automatic, sliding glass door opened. He proceeded through the door and found himself in an exotic rooftop garden enclosed in a green house. Plaques indicated the species and origin of each plant. Henry stopped to examine a bizarre, reddish purple, venous sack, a plant unlike anything he had ever seen.

"*Nepenthes attenboroughii,*" a booming, Yorkshire-accented voice said, "otherwise known as the Rat-Eating Pitcher Plant. The largest meat-eating plant in the world. You would have to go to Mount Victoria in the Philippines to see one in a native environment."

"Hello, Melvin."

Six months had passed since Henry had last seen Entz in person. Entz's forced smile highlighted his wrinkles – the man looked like a Shar Pei with glasses. Henry had once joked to Cheryl that the sum of the folds in Entz's face would add up to his age, like rings on a tree. This year Entz would turn seventy seven.

Henry shook Entz's small, firm hand. "You have quite a garden here. I didn't know you had such a passion for horticulture?"

"Horticulture? My passion is for owning what no one else has."

"Is that why you recruited Chef Shibui to your restaurant? I hear he's one of a kind."

"Ha!" Entz's laugh was a single, staccato note. The burst didn't seem genuine but then, neither was Entz.

Entz led Henry through the main doors of Shibui. "In Japanese, 'shibui' means simplicity, devoid of unnecessary elements. You'll see that the décor within the restaurant has no wasted adornments. Chef Shibui's food will provide all the ornamentation we need."

Bamboo screens separated an otherwise open, large room with high ceilings and bamboo floors. The two men sat down on cushions on the ground on either side of a square, keyaki wood table.

Chef Shibui appeared as soon as they were seated, placing a square, wooden plate in front of each of them. On the plate was an arrangement of delicate, pastel-shaded fish that could have been mounted on a museum wall.

"Toro tartare with caviar," the Chef whispered. He then disappeared back into the kitchen.

"And so begins the Shibui experience. I assume you're content to eat omakase?" Entz asked referring to the Japanese custom of allowing the Chef to determine the menu.

"I wouldn't have it any other way," Henry said.

Shibui was renowned for flying the freshest fish from all over the world to his restaurant on the day of the meal. Dinner at Shibui would last at least three hours.

"I hate to inject such crass matters into such an elegant dining experience, Melvin, but I would be interested in knowing how the recommendations we discussed last time have performed within your organizations."

"Henry my boy, there are only a few things in life more satisfying to me than making money. One of those things is control. Your strategies have given me the ability to control people and thus control outcomes."

"So you're finding the data collection techniques we discussed useful?"

"I know more about my customers now than I do about my own children, Henry. I know. That's a shameless statement. But it's true."

Henry resisted the impulse to ask about his children. He had read gossip reports that he had six or seven from several different women.

"Do you feel you have the competency within your organization to analyze the data?" Henry asked.

"We have a team of statisticians and sociometricians second to none – including three of your former graduate students. They're doing bloody well."

Chef Shibui appeared again from the kitchen. He brought with him their next course.

"Alga, wakame sunomono and grilled octopus with onion caper," the Chef whispered before disappearing again.

Henry typically wasn't fond of octopus but he had faith in Chef Shibui. He lifted a tentacle into his mouth. Shibui's octopus would have been dried and beaten in the sun for nearly an entire day to draw out all of the moisture. A less sophisticated preparation would have left the octopus a rubbery mass. Henry cut Shibui's octopus with a chopstick.

"You realize, your current data collection approaches are a mere shadow of what they could be," Henry said. "Would you like to take Entz Media to the next level?"

"You haven't let me down yet my boy."

Henry signaled Entz to give him a minute before responding. He discretely used his tongue to dislodge an octopus tentacle that had wedged between his teeth.

"The service we're offering is a little different than our other services," Henry said.

"Go on."

"I will offer to expand your data collection methods free of charge if you agree to one thing."

"Quit holding the punch line hostage Henry. Tell me the damage."

"Melvin, I'll show you how to create the most exhaustive information gathering and data analytics services in the world. All *I* want is your data."

Where is the Life
we have lost in living?
Where is the wisdom
we have lost in knowledge?
Where is the knowledge
we have lost in information?

- T.S. Eliot, "The Rock" (1934)

CHAPTER 4

Six Months Later

Laroy Elden was tired of speaking when no one listened.

Well, people did listen. The lecture hall was filled with friendly, supportive faces . . . good people who would go home feeling validated but unimpassioned. He was an excellent speaker. He supported his views with sound logic and relevant statistics. Few people disagreed with Laroy. Even fewer cared.

At seventy-three Laroy wore his age well. His swept back, wispy, white hair framed a set of understanding, kind eyes. Where he was once six feet tall, he now stood an inch or two shorter. He no longer possessed his former muscular frame, but his body was still strong and capable. His mind had never been sharper.

He had been invited to speak at a profamily conference in San Jose, California, preaching to the choir once again. He struggled to find the emotion to present his message with the conviction it deserved.

"Each new generation is a barbarian invasion of an existing, thriving culture. The latest generation requires acculturation, assimilation, and accommodation in order to become productive members of society. If the members of a society fail to pass on the wisdom that underlies that culture's success – wisdom often born out of difficult circumstances and through ponderous reasoning – the very existence of that culture is threatened. Never before has a culture been so challenged as ours in this present day. As stewards of our culture, we have lost the ability to convey wisdom to the stakeholders of the future.

"Although many extol the virtues of our current information age, few comprehend the irony of our day. As a culture we consume more data than at any other time in human history. But has this appetite for information led to an increase in knowledge and ultimately to more wisdom? Or has it simply made us fat, dumb, and satisfied. As it was said about the Romans, so it will be said of us, the only thing of importance was bread and circuses."

Laroy looked into the audience only to see scattered, blank smiling faces staring back at him. He quickened his tempo in an attempt to make his presentation more dynamic.

"Instead of thinking about serious things, we're driven to distraction by gadgetry. We've abdicated our intelligence to technology. We even proudly speak of information stored in the internet cloud as if it was heaven sent. And even if the information provided can be meaningful, many among us have lost the ability to process and contextualize it.

"Studies have shown that college students today are losing the ability to immerse themselves in complex arguments. After a couple of pages, their minds wander as if they are looking for the next hyperlink to relieve their brain of work. These people's brains have become so accustomed to a junk food diet that they have forgotten how to digest sustentative nourishment.

"Ladies and gentlemen, how do you promote morality in a world of sensationalized digital distractions? How do you teach a young man respect for himself and others when he's driven to watch endless internet snippets of people putting themselves in destructive situations? How do you teach a young woman modesty when digital mediums overwhelmingly promote promiscuity? How do you convince young people to forego immediate gratification for a greater future reward when we live in a culture of immediacy? Will we, as a culture, wake up before the consequences of our thoughtless self-indulgence ruin those we care about?"

Laroy paused and then picked up his delivery again with more force and volume.

"We live in a world where love, commitment, and honor have been replaced by sexual exploration, lust, and immorality. One of the most important words in our language, 'marriage' is losing meaning.

"We live in a world where children are being sexualized by so called 'main stream' entertainment and product companies. This is to say nothing about the insidious and disastrous effects of pornography in our society. Pornography has covered our land like a disease and left in its seductive and addictive wake the ruins of broken homes. Recent statistics have shown that our young people are accessing pornography at younger ages. We are also seeing that an increasing number of those addicted to pornography are women.

"The biggest profiteers from pornography are cable and digital satellite companies, whose parent brands are among the most respected in the industry. Executives at these companies have rationalized that, since no consumer outrage has occurred, they are justified in their exploits. After all, everyone needs to turn a profit, right?"

Laroy looked to the audience for a response. He saw a couple of heads nodding in agreement.

"Obscenity laws have been antiquated by our changing technological landscape. The historical obscenity standards set forth in Miller vs. State of California held that 'community standards' decide the type of material that is considered offensive. But in the digital age, which 'community' sets the standards? Virtual communities exist for the sole purpose of mainstreaming even the most deviant of behaviors.

"The effects of prolonged exposure to pornography are many. Those who view pornography have an exaggerated perception of sexual activity in society. They believe that promiscuity is the natural state. And perhaps most troubling of all, those that consume pornography lose the desire to form or maintain families and raise children. Are you content to live in a culture where a loving relationship between a committed mother and father is outdated?"

A man rose from the third row to excuse himself. Laroy paused to allow the distraction to pass.

"The marketers will tell you that 'sex sells.' What they won't tell you is that sex outside of marriage can also destroy. The wisdom of the past is clear on this subject. The eminent historians Will and Ariel Durant, in their book 'The Lessons of History' observed back in 1968:

> 'A youth boiling with hormones will wonder why he should not give full freedom to his sexual desires; and if he is unchecked by custom, morals, or laws, he may ruin his life before he matures sufficiently to understand that sex is a river of fire that must be banked and cooled by a hundred restraints if it is not to consume both the individual and the group' (Will and Ariel Durant, *The Lessons of History* [New York: Simon and Schuster, 1968], pp. 35–36)."

Laroy organized his notes, then set them aside. It was time to talk from the heart.

"As many of you know, I'm a grandfather. I started 'Save Our Families' over twenty years ago when I became convinced that our culture is only as strong as each family unit. I became concerned as I saw how the pervasive use of technology subverted the influence of good families trying to raise decent, well adjusted, contributing children. At that time I was primarily worried about media in general. This was before the advent of the internet, smart phones, social networks, tablet computers, and all the other devices that define our daily life.

"I'm saddened to tell you that as of today, we're losing this battle. Our message of personal responsibility is unpopular. The notion that our country is only as strong as each individual family is unexciting. The warning that the weakest among us are being manipulated for financial gain goes unheeded."

Laroy spotted a couple of empathetic looks from an otherwise preoccupied audience. He then went off script entirely.

"I must leave the charge of carrying on this cause to broader shoulders and more nimble feet than mine. My mediums are outdated and unsophisticated. My reasoning requires contemplation and soul searching. I have been ineffective. My approach was tailored for a former time. This cause now requires a different kind of messenger."

Laroy then put his notes in a briefcase and left the stage, leaving the silent crowd behind him.

It is not from the benevolence
of the butcher, the brewer, or the baker
that we expect our dinner,
but from their regard to their own interest.

- Adam Smith,
"The Wealth of Nations"
(1776, Book I, Chapter II, pg. 19)

CHAPTER 5

Pressley Hamil darted across the Berkeley California campus, weaving through frantic students on her way to the entrance to Wheeler Hall. Her straight, auburn hair extended below a vermillion, knitted cap; just enough to brush against her shoulders. An ivory, crocheted tunic covered a tea green, long sleeve, t-shirt reaching eight inches below her charcoal leggings. Saffron, vintage sneakers punctuated the ensemble. Strangely, the style worked. Pressley detested trendy labels. They were for followers. She wanted to lead.

She made it inside the auditorium but was slowed by a morass of people trying to locate their seats. She knew hesitation could mean loss. Looking towards the back of the auditorium, she spotted a vacancy. Pressley approached the young man next to the empty seat.

"Is this seat taken?" Pressley asked.

The student moved his backpack. "Have at it."

"You'd think they could find a place large enough to handle this crowd," Pressley said.

"Wheeler's the largest auditorium on campus. The craziness should settle down after those wanting to add the class find they're out of luck."

The young man seemed studious, intense but harmless. Most important to Pressley was that he didn't seem like the type of guy who would be throwing pick-up lines at her all class. Pressley had a curious, attainable allure, the type that made every guy she met feel like he had a chance.

"My name's Pressley."

"I'm Thomas. Good to meet you."

As Thomas went to shake Pressley's hand, a newspaper fell to the floor.

"Wow, you don't see many of those anymore. Is that the school newspaper?" Pressley asked.

"Yeah, this could be a collector's edition. The paper will go all digital next semester. I was reviewing one of my articles – I write for them."

"You're a journalism major?"

"So far."

"What made you want to take this class?"

"The teacher makes serious money consulting major corporations," said Thomas. "He's a best-selling author. He's on all of those cable TV talk shows. What's not to like? Do you remember that student who dropped out of school to start that dating website?"

"The one that targeted forty and fifty year-old women wanting to hook-up with younger men? Cougar something dot com?"

"Yeah, well he made a ton of money. In an interview he said this class gave him the inspiration for that business."

"So what you're saying is that every student in here thinks this class will give them their own multimillion dollar idea?"

"Or at least, they recognize this class' value. One semester's tuition couldn't even cover what the Professor charges for one of his weeklong workshops."

Pressley stared at the big screen in front of the auditorium. The screen read:

THE ECONOMICS OF CULTURE
by Dr. Henry Maddox

Seemed like a pretty self-important title for a class.

"Wasn't Dr. Maddox supposed to be here by now?" she said.

"When you're Dr. Maddox, you can pretty much start, finish, or even cancel your class on a whim. The University provides him flexibility, and in return Dr. Maddox strengthens the school's reputation. The college is just happy to have him . . . on any terms."

Just as Thomas finished his comment, the class chatter stopped. Every student's eyes were on the person who came through the door. The man walked with a decided swagger. Not that his entrance needed any more emphasis beyond the sudden reverence that filled the hall.

"Above all things, I'm a capitalist."

The man's wireless microphone projected his soft, relaxed voice through the building.

"In a free market economy, demand is the key – that which sells is produced. Too many people, however, wait for the market to come to them. If you want to make real money, you can't be content to just create products and services to meet the needs of a market. If you want to make real money, you need to learn how to create the markets themselves."

The man bounded up the steps to the stage and turned and faced the students.

"My name is Professor Henry Maddox and this is not your mother's marketing class."

A raucous applause filled the lecture hall. Maddox bathed in it.

"This may not be the most edifying class you take here, but it will certainly be the most useful. I'm not here to tell you heartwarming stories about companies that have changed the world. I'm here to teach you how to make money. You'll probably find that you resist many of the concepts we explore in this class. That's fine. While you wrestle with the moral implications of such ideas, your classmates will make a fortune implementing them. If this disturbs you, you're free to withdraw. As you can see from the crowd assembled, there's a line of other students waiting to take your seat."

Maddox paced across the stage. He clicked a remote and a massive image of a man in a powdered wig appeared on the screen behind him.

"A free market economy is driven by motive. The economist Adam Smith called this motive the 'invisible hand.' It's why persons and businesses do what they do. Except for certain virtuous exceptions, people will always pursue their own self-interest."

Pressley began typing notes into her laptop.

"Why would an eight o'clock TV show targeting teens – during television's so called 'family hour' – push the boundaries of teenage sexuality?" Maddox asked. "Could it be because there's money in teen sexuality? If you can convince a teenager that she should define herself by how desirable she is, isn't it easier to sell to her? Next time you watch one of these shows, take note of the advertisements – chewing gum for fresh breath, acne creams, even shoes that will tone your backside.

"But how did we get to the super charged consumer economy in which we currently live? Let's rewind the clock a bit . . ."

"After World War II, America experienced an economic boom. During war time, consumers delayed purchases and the private sector dedicated resources to supporting the war effort. After the war, the private sector began producing cars, homes, and consumer electronics. And consumers' appetites increased.

"Prior to 1946, young people generally worked to help support their own families. Families didn't have much disposable income, so the entire family income typically went to necessities. This was especially the case in agricultural areas, which were the norm prior to the mechanization of farming in the twenties."

A portrait of a boy dressed in a new suit leaving his family's farm to go to college flashed on the screen. The rancher dad was dressed in blue jeans and a denim shirt. The father showed no emotion. A sad collie rested his head on the boy's knee.

"This painting is titled 'Breaking Home Ties,' and was painted by Norman Rockwell in 1954."

Sympathetic expressions were heard throughout the crowd.

"Fast forward to the 1950s, a new consumer group was born . . . the teenager. With young people now working outside of the home, and with families now having an increased amount of discretionary purchasing power, the teenager was now spending money on his own wants. Not on his family's needs. So on which items do you think teenagers spent their money?"

The class was silent.

"That wasn't rhetorical. I'm actually looking for an answer. We can't have a discussion if no one participates."

A flurry of students' hands went up in the air.

"Feel free to shout out the answers," Dr. Maddox said.

"Poodle skirts," someone said.

"Leather jackets," someone else said.

"Burgers, fries, and shakes at the malt shop," another student said.

"Congratulations, I can see you've either seen the musical Grease or watched the TV show Happy Days. The reality is that an endless stream of products and services entered the market. From Hula Hoops to Yo-Yos to blue jeans, the free market recognized the seemingly limitless potential of exploiting the teenager for profit.

"To someone studying consumerism, the 1950s was the beginning of something big – *market fragmentation*. A previously homogeneous market had now been separated into at least two pieces – the family being one piece and the teenager being the other. As marketers drove the wedge between the family and the teenager deeper, greater market potential emerged. The family and the teenager began to have increasingly distinct preferences. Marketers employed the new mediums of television, film, and rock and roll music to accelerate the notion that the teenager should rebel against his out-of-touch parents."

Maddox clicked a remote control that projected a movie clip onto the screen. An emotional young man in the 1950s was sitting at a table.

"You're tearing me apart!"
"What?" The mother asked.
"You say one thing and then he says another (pointing to the father) and then everybody changes back again!"

Maddox clicked the remote again to pause the video.

"That's a clip from the now legendary 1950s film 'Rebel Without A Cause,' with the iconic James Dean as the son. Just one of many forms of media that promoted family discord as a main plot line."

Students pounded on their keyboards and then clicked on various links to find the referenced movie.

"Creating the distinct teenage market was a profound advance in marketing," Maddox said, "and it provided a vision of how to fragment other markets."

A PowerPoint slide now appeared on the screen.

To successfully fragment a market, a business must do the following:

1) Identify a market that has high disposable income characteristics (i.e. market opportunity).

2) Figure out a way to fragment that market into at least two distinct segments.

3) Use advertising mediums to define characteristics of the new market fragments.

4) Produce products or services to meet the needs of these new market segments.

"Can you think of other examples of how fragmentation has led to increased market opportunity?" Maddox asked. "Anyone?"

"What about dual income families?" a student asked.

"Keep going."

A young lady ten or fifteen rows in front of Pressley stood up. "Well, for years the traditional family consisted of a working father and a stay-at-home mother. In today's culture this is more the exception than the norm. How much of this evolution to having two incomes is out of necessity and how much of it is to satisfy wants rather than needs?"

"I'm not going to let you off that easily. Guide me through the steps."

"Okay, I'll try. First, marketers determined that, if they could convince both the husband and the wife to work, the household would have more disposable income. This establishes the market opportunity criteria. Second, marketers figured out a way to fragment the traditional concept of a stay-at-home mother by promoting the idea of fulfillment through one's career. I don't know the advertising strategy behind all of this, but it seems that today stay-at-home mothers are meant to feel less than working mothers. Third, advertisers always show that working mothers wear nice clothes to work, have nice homes, drive nice cars, and eat out at nice restaurants. This is a much sexier lifestyle than staying at home, making peanut butter and jelly sandwiches, and hoping to get a few moments in the day where you can take a five minute shower."

Some chuckles spread through the audience.

"And the fourth criteria?" Maddox asked.

"Well this is easy – it relates to number three. Working mothers need new, expensive clothes. They probably eat out much more since they aren't home for lunch and probably don't have as much time to cook dinner. They need a nice car to drive, since the family minivan doesn't command much respect at the office. Working women need pedicures and manicures. They visit the hair salon much more frequently. A working woman is not afraid to spend money on herself, since *she* earned the money. And, a working woman will spoil her children by buying them lots of clothes and toys and taking them on vacations, to the movies, or to amusement parks (when they do have time off) because she feels guilty about spending so much time away from them."

The young lady was smiling by the time she finished, but the smile melted when she realized that most of the class was shooting daggers at her.

"Why is everyone staring down our friend over here?" Maddox asked. "Is it politically incorrect to assert that working women try to compensate for their physical absence in their children's lives by buying their affection? Or is it simple fact?"

Another young woman stood up. "It seems irresponsible to generalize that all working women have been manipulated by savvy marketers. Doesn't that minimize their contribution to society? I can't believe that all working women have been duped into the workforce by corporations for the sole reason of wanting to exploit a new market segment."

"Why not?" Maddox asked. "Just because the thought makes you uncomfortable doesn't mean it's incorrect. I'm not saying that working women are not competent or that they don't make a valuable contribution in the workforce. They are and they do. But the very fact that your emotions won't allow you to entertain this possibility is proof that the *market fragmentation* has been successful. I'm certain that, as we identify other market fragments, almost everyone in here will be offended. Why? Because up to this point you've convinced yourself that you are who you are because you decided to be that way. I view the world differently. You see independence and originality among your peers. I see fragments that have been manipulated for profit.

"Remember, I'm a capitalist. I identify and exploit profit opportunities. The invisible hand has fragmented the single income household. All the politically correct language in the world won't change that. While you're distracted by the unseemliness of this assertion, I'll make money off of the fragmented consumer group."

Pressley had stopped taking notes some time ago. It just couldn't be possible that society was so completely shaped by the need of corporations to make a profit. People just weren't so easily controlled.

"Market fragmentation is a deliberate and calculated process," Maddox said. "I should know. Companies pay me a lot of money to show them how to do it. The infant stages of the fragmentation are the most critical. When a market begins to fragment, social philosopher types always question whether such an evolution is healthy for our culture. As a capitalist, I want to get through this stage quickly – get the horse out of the barn so to speak – so that the incentives are so strong to perpetuate the fragmentation that any discussion over whether dual income households are good for society (for example) is irrelevant. The fragmentation is considered necessary."

Maddox removed his cufflinks, placing them in his pocket, and rolled up the sleeves of his shirt. "Once corporations manufacture goods and produce services for new market segments, they validate the cultural fragmentation through comprehensive media campaigns.

Given that 90 percent of what we read, watch, or listen to comes from only six media giants, this process has grown progressively easier and much more effective.

"These types of media campaigns now have the power to overwhelm the social philosopher types," Maddox said. "After all, who will give the social philosophers air time when the advertisers control the airwaves? Where is the money in preserving tradition? It doesn't matter how valid their arguments are if no one hears them. And even if the social philosopher could find a platform, the newest hip sitcom, movie, or magazine articles will make a much more persuasive argument than any reasoned logic could provide. Rational debate takes work, the masses want entertainment. The new fragmented social segment thus quickly becomes accepted and exploited."

Maddox walked to the edge of the stage and signaled to the young lady who made the initial comment about dual income households. "When was the last time you saw a stay-at-home mom as a main character in a television show or movie? When was the last time that stay-at-home moms were exalted rather than debased in the media? As a marketer, I want stay-at-home moms to be portrayed as having settled for less than what they could have become. A storyline would say that a woman's *real dream* was to chase some satisfying career but things didn't work out so she became *only* a stay-at-home mom."

"Hold on," a young man said, "stay-at-home moms buy a lot of stuff – diapers, food, clothing, detergent, all sorts of home necessities. Doesn't a profit motive also exist for keeping a mother in the home? I see commercials all the time that have stay-at-home moms washing their kid's clothes with a certain brand of detergent or taking their kids to soccer practice in a certain style of minivan."

"Good point," Dr. Maddox said, "let's study that dynamic a little further. Generally, working moms have the same consumption needs as stay-at-home moms. If you have kids, you're buying clothes, food, detergent, and such whether you're a working mom or a stay-at-home mom. The real question is, do you want a consumer with more money or less money? As a producer of goods and services, I want a mom that has more income and I don't want them to save that income, I want them to spend it.

"Now let's shift to another target for market fragmentation. What if you could divide a home? If a mother and father split, each new home will be forced to buy twice as much to satisfy their needs."

"Whoa," the same student said, "so now you're saying that companies selling detergent, homes, or other household items want to see married couples divorce?"

"Divorce? Sure that would be good. It would also be good if they never marry. The traditional family is the least attractive market segment. Traditional families are cost efficient and typically more prudent with their financial resources. I want a market segment that's irresponsible, whimsical, and selfish, that will buy on impulse with their extra money or even go into debt to finance an unnecessary purchase. Don't you guys watch TV, read magazines, or listen to pop music? Why do you think that the programming is so sexed up? Nothing breaks up a family faster than pervasive sexuality. You can break up a husband

and a wife. You can cause a boyfriend and girlfriend not to make a lasting commitment to each other because of an unrealistic relationship expectation. You can even poison the children in a family so they have unhealthy attitudes towards sex. As marketers, we promote sex as natural and fun, but we never talk about responsibility or consequences – that's boring and unproductive. Remember, we don't want responsible consumers; we want thoughtless, emotional ones.

"Consider one of my favorite marketing gems of all time. How often have you heard the idea that a married couple divorced because 'they fell out of love?' You see, as marketers, we can promote an idealized – and unobtainable – image of a marital relationship. Soon each partner in a marriage begins to think they're missing out on something. We incorporate story lines in movies and television shows where people 'fall out of love.' We can run articles in magazines and newspapers about what it means to 'fall in love.' We take reason out of the equation. We convince people that no one decides to love. Couples must fall helplessly into a relationship. This way, they can just as easily fall out.

"So the answer is yes. We as marketers can and do break up marriages. We orchestrate the message through several different mediums simultaneously so that divorce appears to be easy and normal. And yes breaking families apart is good for business."

A large quote was displayed on the screen in back of Maddox.

"The better is the enemy of the good."

"These lines were penned by an eighteenth century French writer and philosopher named Francois-Marie Arouet, more commonly known by his pen name, Voltaire. Little did Voltaire know that the reverse of this statement would be the foundation of all marketing ploys. Our modern marketing mantra has become: 'never be satisfied.' People who are content are of no use to us. Consumers who are unsatisfied can be manipulated. In the marketing world, we want to constantly make people feel unfulfilled and miserable.

"We're running out of time today so let me give you your homework assignment. Look at everything you do over the next couple of days: the TV shows you watch, the music you listen to, the material you read, etc. and ask yourself how these influences are shaping who you are. Then ask yourself, who is profiting from this person that I'm becoming? You'll be surprised at what you find."

I kissed a girl just to try it
I hope my boyfriend don't mind it
It felt so wrong
It felt so right
Don't mean I'm in love tonight

- Katy Perry, "I Kissed a Girl" (2008)
Nominated for Favorite Song
at the 2009 Kids' Choice Awards

CHAPTER 6

Pressley and Thomas pushed through the crowd until they finally burst through the doors and onto the wide steps.

"How many students do you think were in there?" Pressley asked.

"Including the standing room onlies at the back? Probably a couple thousand I'd guess." Thomas said.

"Why would Professor Maddox give away his money making marketing strategies to students – for free – when he could be charging corporations boat loads of money? Seems a little odd, doesn't it?"

"The information he shares in class is probably Maddox 101. I'm sure he has many more advanced tactics he gives to his clients. These classroom lectures are mere appetizers –

they just build anticipation towards the seminars, which people pay big money for."

A lot of what Professor Maddox had said was still sinking in. Could her life really be so thoroughly determined by advertising? "I think I'm content with the appetizers for now."

"Well, whatever Maddox's motive, people make lots of money using his advice. When people make money, they don't ask questions."

"Guess you're right."

"And on an interesting note, some of Maddox's former students – Jeff Hoffman and Harmony Winter, for instance – are now trying to compete with Maddox in the same consulting space. Even Maddox needs to continue to evolve his strategies to stay ahead of his competitors."

So for all his talk about the profit motive, he was giving away his secrets essentially for free and creating his own competition. She wasn't sure if this was just normal, human contradiction or if there was something more devious.

"Hey listen," Thomas said. "If you ever want to get together and study, let me know."

"Okay, thanks. I live off campus though so usually it's kind of hard to get together with people."

Thomas's face fell. "No worries. I understand."

"It's just that if I didn't live off campus, it would be a lot easier to get together." Pressley scrambled trying to make her excuse not sound like a rejection. "I would appreciate you saving me a seat for next class, though."

"Fair enough. I'll be in charge of the seats," Thomas said, his half grin turning to a full smile.

For the first time Pressley noticed Thomas' deep brown, sincere eyes through his black rimmed glasses. He seemed nice. Maybe it was time she gave a nice guy a chance.

"Well, I better get going. I've got a train to catch," Pressley said. "See you later."

"Later."

Pressley turned and raced down the path to the off–campus Bay Area Rapid Transit stop. Once Thomas was out of sight, her thoughts returned to Maddox's lecture. Was there some conspiracy to shape her behavior by powerful business interests? What did these corporate titans want her to become?

Pressley boarded BART, found a seat by herself, placed her bags beside her, and prepared to relax. She pulled out her iPhone and chose one of her audio playlists. The upbeat song began to pulsate through her headphones. Pressley had heard the song many times before but never focused on the lyrics. As she listened, the words in the song now had a special bite to them.

> "We drove to Cali and got drunk on the beach
> Got a motel and built a floor out of sheets
> I finally found you, my missing puzzle piece
> I'm complete
>
> Let's go all the way tonight
> No regrets, just love
> We can dance until we die
> You and I, we'll be young forever"
> (Katy Perry, "Teenage Dream")

Pressley had seen preteen girls dancing to this song before and thought nothing of it. What message was being provided to these young girls? Get drunk, get a motel room, go all the way? What was the justification? No regrets, just love because they'll be young forever. The message was clear: live for the moment and pay no attention to consequences.

Pressley advanced her playlist again.

"No matter gay, straight, or bi
Lesbian, transgendered life
I'm on the right track, baby
I was born to survive

Ooh, there aint no other way, baby, I was born this way . . ."
(Lady Gaga, "Born This Way")

This time the message of the song appeared to be one of accepting who you were born to be. Fair enough. Pressley believed everyone was unique. Why not celebrate it? In listening more intently, however, the message became much more specific. The song championed different types of sexual behaviors as in-born and needing expression. How would young people know if they were gay, straight, or bi unless they took the time to indulge in each of these different behaviors? This was not some obscure song heard in some dance club, however. This song was played frequently on main stream pop radio and listened to by moms driving their young kids to soccer. Considering that these songs reached people as young as eight years-old – before they even had a rudimentary understanding of sexuality – these songs seemed predatory.

Following Dr. Maddox's steps, Pressley took out her laptop and began to document a potential market fragmentation strategy relating to sexualizing young people through music.

1) Identify a market that has high disposable income characteristics (i.e. market opportunity)

   Young people don't make much money. But if it's true that working mothers and fathers spoil their children to make up for lost personal time . . . then the source of the income could be the parent. The manipulation of the child is enabled by the guilt of the parent. Given the amount of media focused on this young age group, companies must recognize this as an extremely important consumer demographic.

2) Figure out a way to fragment that market into at least two distinct segments

   Make children see themselves as sexual from a very early age. The basic fragmentation would be from normal young people to sexual young people. As the children get older, the fragmentation would evolve into sexual identity, which would at the very least be broken into gay, straight, or bi.

3) Use advertising mediums to define characteristics of the new market fragments

Musicians and other celebrities serve as the standard bearers for this hyper sexualized market fragment. In addition to sexualized lyrics, music icons wear overtly sexual apparel and live pleasure-seeking lifestyles that are captured and promoted in gossip news programming. Since many young people don't watch TMZ, they would be targeted indirectly. As parents listened to the radio or leave the television on in the home, the lifestyles of these celebrities would become part of the child's consciousness. Always wanting to appear more adult, these children would then impress their classmates with their knowledge of these pop icon's grownup behaviors. When a classmate shows up in hip, new, celebrity-inspired fashion or sings a sexually explicit song, the fragmentation has taken root.

4) Produce products or services to meet the needs of these new market segments.

Once a person is sexualized, they become a marketable product. Young people would be made to think that their value was based on a certain ideal of physical beauty. As these young people's comparisons to the ideal resulted in feelings of inadequacy, companies would eagerly sell products to compensate for the child's perceived deficiencies.

Pressley thought of a recent news story of a clothier who sold padded bikinis to prepubescent girls and started to feel ill. What type of culture thrusts young children into a sexualized world? Pressley remembered her own teenage years, when she kept comparing her body to those of runway models. What if girls started to worry about that as young as eight years old?

Professor Maddox's words rang in her ears. "You're living the life corporate interests want you to live . . . and as is the motive of all good marketers, they've made you unsatisfied and miserable."

The train pulled into the Concord station at 5:22 p.m. If Pressley hurried, she could still make dinner with her family. She hopped on her used, Honda scooter. All she needed was a way to get from her home to the BART station, and the scooter was the cheapest solution. The high pitched whiz of the engine made her feel like she was going much faster than the 30 miles per hour her speedometer showed, an apt metaphor for her life. Although she was busy, she felt like she was going nowhere.

Pressley pulled into the driveway. The commute from Martinez to Berkeley each day was a killer, especially during rush hour. Living at home also meant she didn't enjoy the same celebrated, college social life as some of her peers. But it saved her money – she'd calculated that, even living at home, she would have about one hundred thousand dollars in student debt by the time she graduated. In her sober moments she felt overwhelmed by the obligation. Other people were doing it though, right? Once she started earning a paycheck the debt wouldn't seem like such a big deal. Or so she hoped.

But there is a difficulty
about disagreeing with God.
He is the source from which
 all your reasoning power comes...

- C.S. Lewis, The Case for Christianity

CHAPTER 7

As was his practice, Laroy Elden woke early. The quiet of the predawn morning was a perfect time for solitude and reflection. Every morning, he left his bedroom to go to his study, opened the blinds in anticipation of the sun's morning rays, and knelt by his chair to pray. Laroy's prayers were conversational. He spoke to God as if he were a friend. At times he would get upset at God, and was willing to make his complaints known. Many more orthodox believers would have considered his prayers disrespectful, but he figured an all-powerful, omniscient God could handle whatever little Laroy could throw at him. Besides, anything less than full honesty would not only be disingenuous, it would be pointless. God knew his heart, so why pretend?

Theoretically prayer was a form of reconciliation between his will and God's will. In practice, however, prayer for Laroy was more like a wrestling match. He knew that God's way was perfect, but it was often hard not to feel God should move more in his direction. He felt comfort in thinking that he was asking the right questions, but he also experienced immense frustration at the timing and content of God's answers.

This morning's prayer was a watershed – he was handing God his resignation. He had dedicated twenty years of his life to strengthening communities by protecting the family. He had fought admirably, but now it was time for others more capable than him to take up the cause.

Satisfied, he arose from his knees, sat down at his desk, and resumed reading in the Bible where he had left off the day before – the fourteenth chapter of Matthew. Laroy read of how Christ grieved over Herod having beheaded His cousin, John the Baptist. Jesus wanted to be alone and sought "a desert place apart" (v: 13) but many people followed Him. Sensing the needs of these people, Christ was "moved with compassion" and healed their sick (v: 14). Laroy reflected on how Jesus, the perfect example, reached out to help others despite his own suffering.

But how to apply this to his own circumstances? He was tired and frustrated at what he felt was God's mission for him. He, like Christ in the passage, wanted to be left alone. Christ's love ultimately overcame His need to grieve, however. Could Laroy's love provide the added motivation to continue with his cause? But what would be the use if those he loved still wouldn't listen?

Laroy went back to the passage. After healing many, Christ multiplied five loaves of bread and two fishes to feed "about five thousand men, beside women and children" (v.

16 – 21). If he came closer to Christ, could He multiply Laroy's humble offering the same way that He multiplied the five loaves and two fishes?

Laroy continued reading. After feeding the five thousand, Christ asked His disciples to get into a ship and to go before Him while he went to a mountain to pray alone. In Christ's absence the disciples became frightened as the waves and wind tossed them about on the waters. In the "fourth watch of the night" – which would have been the hours just before dawn – "Jesus went unto them, walking on the sea." Laroy was humbled. Christ allowed His disciples to endure the storm for almost the whole night before intervening. As a follower of Christ, Laroy could expect no different. Christ would save him from his challenges on His timeframe – usually after much anxiety and discomfort, but always for a purpose.

So . . . he had the answer to his prayer. God had rejected his resignation. Laroy would now need to pray for miracles, not validation.

The first beams of sunlight crested over the foothills, casting shadows on the walls of his study. It was time for Laroy to prepare for another day.

Laroy strained to make eye contact with the boy's sunken gaze. His colorless skin and frail body slumped in the chair.

"How are you enjoying your time here at New Beginnings?" Laroy asked.

Silence pervaded the room, and Laroy let it bloom. In polite conversation, the quiet would have been uncomfortable. But this dialog was more an exercise than an exchange of information.

An entire minute passed.

"Benjamin, what did you think of the hike in the mountains yesterday?" Laroy asked.

The boy surveyed the room without meeting Laroy's eyes, and then looked at the floor. "I got hot and thirsty. And tired. How much longer do I have to be here?"

"You're doing great, Ben. Now try to look at me when you're speaking to me."

The boy looked at Laroy, examined his appearance, and then lost interest.

"How long have you been here Benjamin?"

"About five days."

"How long do you plan on staying?"

Benjamin began to squirm. "I'm here for a total of forty five days."

"Have you set some goals for yourself while you're here?"

"Kind of."

"What types of goals are you thinking about?"

"The counselors want me to manage my time and keep a schedule. They want me to learn how to make and keep friends. They want me to learn how to talk to people better."

"Is this what you want?"

"No not really. I just want to go home."

"Well, you'll go home soon enough. Try to enjoy your time while you're here. This is a special place, and I know everyone here cares about you. Do you feel that?"

"Feel what?"

"That the people here care about you?"

"Sure, I guess."

"Well . . . just take one day at a time. Don't get too overwhelmed, okay? This whole program is meant to improve your life. I know that if you do what's asked of you, you'll leave here a happier person."

A knock on the window caused Laroy to look up. A counselor waved him out of the room.

"That means my time's up. Thanks for spending time talking to me, Benjamin. Would it be all right if I came back to see you again sometime?"

"They don't let me decide," Benjamin said.

"I understand. Take care of yourself."

Laroy left the room and was greeted by the facility manager, Mrs. Jennifer Bennett.

"Thank you for volunteering, Mr. Elden," Jennifer said. "We try to bring in people from the outside at least once a week to talk to our patients."

"So you do describe your clients as patients?"

"Loosely. We have board supervised counselors, psychologists, and psychiatrists that work with us. In that context, our clients are patients. Internet addiction still hasn't been officially classified as a distinct clinical disorder, however, so our clients don't have a recognized medical diagnosis. I guess the larger medical community may disagree with our use of the term."

"But you see this changing?"

"The United States is actually behind the curve on treating these types of stimulus addictions. China, Taiwan, and South Korea have all identified internet addiction as national problems among their youth. Americans are just now waking up to the fact."

Laroy looked back to the room where Benjamin was doubtless still sitting staring at the wall. It was like there was no one home. "Just what happened to Benjamin?"

"It's classic withdrawal. Before his parents brought him in, he had become so engrossed in video gaming that he never came out of his room. His parents would knock on the door and put a plate of food by it so he would break for meals. Often he didn't. Ben would play his games through the night to the exclusion of sleep. He soon grew too tired to go to school and he dropped out. Out of desperation, his parents contacted us."

"Why wouldn't his parents have just taken his gaming system out of his room?"

"He still would have faced withdrawal, but he would have been doing it alone. Back in 2011, the American Society of Addiction Medicine issued a public statement defining all addiction in terms of brain changes. In fact, where it typically takes five to seven days for someone with a chemical addiction to purge the chemical from the body, it can take anywhere from thirty to sixty days to detox a process addict. A process addict has actually had his brain physically changed. To detox, you need to remove the stimuli and through different therapies readjust the brain back to normal dopamine levels."

"So Ben's parents were afraid of the withdrawal symptoms? Could they have been much worse than his addiction symptoms?"

"Easily. Depression, anxiety, and maladjustment to reality so severe the addict becomes desperate – and often dangerous – to soothe them. Internet addicts need to be brought to the point where they reengage with reality. That is where we come in. We teach our clients life skills so they can begin to experience real world success again. We get them to exercise so that increased oxygenation to the brain can begin to repair neural pathways. We also conduct cognitive exercises so the brain begins to reestablish connections that may have been lost. We reintroduce them to nature, to healthy relationships, productive hobbies. We want the satisfaction of actual achievement to replace – excuse me for one second, Mr. Elden."

Jennifer stepped away to review some patient information with an attendant who had been trying to get her attention. Within a couple of minutes she returned.

"I'm sorry, Mr. Elden, where were we?"

"You're fine, Jennifer. We were talking about Benjamin and process addiction. Is it more than gaming?"

"Usually, at least with teenage boys and men – online gaming and pornography. Recently we're seeing teenage girls with some of the same problems, but among women, it's more likely to be online shopping and social networking. Online gambling is a problem for both genders. And the addictions aren't mutually exclusive – gaming may lead to pornography or social networking addiction may lead to online shopping. The key addictive trait is that the online addiction manipulates the rewards centers in the brain much like a drug. Once users experience digital highs, they lose interest in real life.

"When patients come to us, it's usually because they've hit rock bottom. They drop out of school and have no real social interactions, like Ben. They become so engrossed in their online behavior that they don't have anything left over for their families or their work. Online addicts usually end up alone, sick, and broke . . . much like substance abuse addicts. If they're lucky, we get to them first. Remind me again of the nature of your interest in our clinic, Mr. Elden?"

"Well . . . I like Ben and would like to see him recover. But I'm also interested in how digital media is breaking apart existing families and keeping new families from forming."

"Oh that's right, you're with Save Our Families. Good cause. We find our patients who don't return to stable family units have a much higher incidence of relapse. As we say in the field, 'neurons that fire together, wire together.' Constant interactions with loved ones are essential in maintaining one's process addiction recovery. We also know that, without loving and supportive families, few of our patients would ever even make it to us."

"Jennifer, is there a solution to this?"

"Well, we can't turn off the internet, and I wouldn't want to. It's amazing in many ways. But there are people – companies, actually – that purposefully addict children to digital mediums for profit. They are no better than corporate drug dealers. I wish I could have one of these people sit down with the families of my patients and feel of their despair. I want them to look into the eyes of a kid who has lost hope and admit to them that they made money on his suffering."

And there it was. Laroy had the second answer to his prayers.

Watch out,
you might get what you're after
Cool babies,
strange but not a stranger
I'm an ordinary guy
Burning down the house

- The Talking Heads
"Burning Down the House" (1983)

CHAPTER 8

An energy existed in Professor Maddox's class like none other on campus. Students discussed how Maddox had changed their view of the world long into the night. They finally knew what it was like to enjoy learning. More than anything else, students talked about money – about companies that used Maddox's tactics and their astronomical net worth. They talked about Maddox's cars – the internet showed the list price on his fully loaded, 5.2 liter Audi R8 at around $200,000; his Mercedes G550 SUV around $100,000. One student had heard that Maddox owned at least two homes, one in San Francisco and another in Lake Tahoe. A friend had driven past the home in San Francisco and spoke of the location, the view, and the size; that given the price of other homes in the neighborhood it must have cost him at least $20 million.

To indebted college students, Professor Maddox's marketing secrets represented a hope of having their educational investment pay off. After History, Humanities, and all of the other impractical prerequisite classes, his students finally were learning something useful. They were learning how to get rich.

The roar of music through the auditorium speakers silenced the students' conversations. The pupils scrambled to reach their seats. The music gave the class a tent-meeting revival feel. The evangelist had won his converts. These disciples were now ready for another sermon.

And Henry was ready to give it to them.

He entered the auditorium from one of the rear hallways and began dancing down the aisle to the music. Delighted students cheered him on. By nature, Henry was reserved, deliberate, but he had taught himself to become more extroverted when he needed to be. There was an irony in cultivating a precisely calculated spontaneity, but he was comfortable with irony. Like now. Every move had been examined and scripted for a single end – to endear him to his audience. With each side step and every twirl, he burrowed himself further into his students' hearts. Sales data showed that people were more likely to buy from people or companies they liked, and Henry *was* selling a philosophy. These students would become his minions to the world's markets.

A final spin put him behind the lectern just as the music ended. No need for preliminaries. He already had their attention.

"Some would say my market fragmentation strategies have destroyed many a home by separating families and communities," he said. "These sentimentalists fail to understand one of the key aspects of free market economics – there *is* profit in dysfunction. Although I would love to take credit for this insight, the notion predates me by centuries. One adherent of this philosophy, Bernard De Mandeville, published a poem titled, 'The Grumbling Hive, or Knaves Turn'd Honest' in the year of our Lord, 1714. This poem has since come to be known as 'The Fable of The Bees.' Quoting from Mandeville:

> Thus every Part was full of Vice,
> Yet the whole Mass a Paradise;
> Flatter'd in Peace,
> And fear'd in Wars,
> They were th' Esteem of Foreigners,
> And lavish of their Wealth and Lives,
> The Balance of all other Hives.
>
> Such were the Blessings of that State;
> Their Crimes conspir'd to make them Great:
> And Virtue, who from Politicks Had learn'd
> A Thousand Cunning Tricks,
> Was, by their happy Influence,
> Made Friends with Vice:
> And ever since,

The worst of all the Multitude
Did something for the Common Good

"Mandeville's fable showed how private vices led to a public benefit. Vices employed people and stimulated the creation of wealth. In fact, when Mandeville's bees decided to seek virtue rather than personal gain at the expense of others, the colony lost their hive.

"The same is true in our world. Without disease, what need would we have of doctors? Without disputes, what need would we have of the judicial system? Without crime, what need would we have for law enforcement? Dysfunction employs people and causes money to circulate. This money creates demand for products and stimulates the economy.

"Now don't misunderstand me. I'm not saying you should go out and literally burn down your neighborhood to stimulate the construction industry – though a couple of centuries ago a French politician named M.F. Chamans did make the argument that burning down Paris would stimulate trade. The position I defend is that people should have as many consumption alternatives as possible. Each alternative should compete on merit. Whether an alternative is ultimately good or bad for a given consumer is not my business. The market will decide the winners and losers. Welcome to America."

Scattered cheers erupted through the auditorium.

"In our last class, we talked about how to create markets. I asked each of you to consider how you've been shaped by consumer culture. Does anyone care to share some of their insights? Yes, the young lady in the back."

Henry signaled Jason, his teaching assistant, to walk the mobile microphone to the rear of the auditorium.

The young lady took a deep breath and straightened her notes.

"Professor Maddox, I spent quite a bit of time–"

"I'm sorry, your name please?"

"Oh. Pressley Hamil. I spent a lot of time researching the effects of media on young adults. The data is staggering. As of 2011, the children's product industry was worth $17 billion. Companies were working day and night to bypass parents and target children directly. Some of the products mentioned in the story include thong underwear for ten year-old girls and a new line of make-up for eight to twelve year-old girls. The article continued to point out that doctors are now seeing anorexia in kids as young as eight or nine years old. How do you reconcile your advocacy of unchecked free markets with the sexualization of these young girls?"

The auditorium fell silent. Students glared at Pressley.

"Please be respectful of the young lady's question," Henry said. "Free speech works both ways, ladies and gentlemen and I always appreciate the opportunity to better clarify my positions. Okay . . . Pressley is it? If you don't mind, may I ask you a couple of questions?"

"Yes sir."

"Did the article you read cite any organizations?"

"Organizations?"

"Yes, did the article quote representatives from any profamily organizations for example?"

"Yes, a couple of representatives from different organizations were quoted."

"And what was the tone of the sentiments expressed by these organizations?"

"They were outraged that corporations were so socially irresponsible."

"Of course. And well they should be, when evil corporations target young, innocent girls. But . . . whom did this article benefit?"

"Benefit?"

"Yes, every action has a motive. Who benefited from this article?"

"I suppose the article allowed profamily organizations to publicize their cause."

"That's one. Who else?"

"Well, the news organization that carried the story benefited, since I actually read the story."

"Certainly, and you could further extend that to the advertisers on the website whose ads you saw, correct?"

"Sure."

"Anyone else?"

"Well, those merchants who were selling the thong underwear and makeup for young girls got some publicity as well."

"Okay, good. So the profamily organizations received publicity that will probably lead to donations. The news organization and advertisers profited off of the visibility of this story. Even the demonized merchants benefited from this story, as they increased their brand awareness. Now for the important question: who was harmed by this story?"

"Well, the story didn't harm anyone. But the products harm the young girls by sexualizing them."

"Do they?"

"I'm not sure that I understand your question."

"Does the fact these products exist present a danger to the young girls, or is it the actual purchasing and wearing of such products that present the harm you're alleging?"

"Well, it would be the purchasing and wearing of such products that would present the danger."

"Then would it not be the parents who purchase the products who are to blame?"

"The parents wouldn't purchase them if they didn't exist, though."

"True enough. But the items do exist. And in a free market economy, producers are free to make those products that people consume. Of course some legal restrictions exist, but in this instance, the merchants are perfectly within the bounds of the law, are they not?"

"Well, yes."

"So it appears the solution to the problem lies in either outlawing the products or encouraging the parents not to buy the items. Which solution are you advocating Pressley?"

"To be honest Professor, I haven't thought through the consequences of either alternative."

"Well, if you outlaw the products, you'll need to hire people to enforce those laws. These new law enforcers would be paid out of taxpayer dollars. So this alternative would increase your taxes, which is never a popular solution. Furthermore, there's the problem of drafting an effective preventative law. At what age should girls be allowed to wear make-up or thong underwear? Would girls be stopped on the street if they were found to be violating the law? Would parents need to fill out a form at the point of purchase certifying that the wearer of the product was of legal age?

"You see, Pressley, I'm not denying that you've put your finger on a real problem. But there is only one answer to the problem. Parents must be parents. Until this occurs, businesses will continue to produce what they can sell. Let's give a hand for the young lady's participation."

The crowd began to applaud, but Pressley remained standing. And when Jason approached her for the microphone, she refused to hand it over.

"Professor," she said, "I have one more question for you. How will parents be parents as you suggest if the family has been fragmented?"

Ooh, a smart one. He loved smart ones. They were so much more interesting than the usual sheep.

"So if I might rephrase," he said, "I'm saying that parents should police their children's behavior better, but at the same advocating marketing strategies that break apart the family."

"Giving predatory corporations an unfair advantage, yes, exactly."

"Are you asking marketers and corporations to have a conscience Pressley?"

"Well, someone certainly should."

"Perhaps, but history has shown the fallacy of expecting that ideal from corporations. Businesses will always migrate to money, regardless of the morality. If consumers really cared about what you've said, they would mobilize and expose these so called predatory companies. You see, consumers ultimately have the power Pressley, and with it, the responsibility. Don't blame evil corporations or marketers like me. How do you guys put it? Don't hate the player, hate the game?"

Nervous laughter echoed through the auditorium.

Pressley handed the microphone back to Jason and then sat down.

"Thank you for your participation Pressley," Henry said. "Really, you've made the class more interesting."

"That isn't exactly how I saw things playing out." Pressley whispered to Thomas under the polite applause. "I just played right into his hands."

"You did fine," Thomas said. "You raised a legitimate concern and even pressed him on his response. I think you'd make a good journalist. Or even better, a good marketer. Think about it, now the entire class knows your name. You're a brand, now. Maybe you could enlist Professor Maddox's help in expanding your market?"

Pressley laughed. "Very funny."

Maddox walked to the front of his stage and addressed the students.

"This bright young lady brought up several arguments I hear a lot. Some would argue that I should feel guilty for employing marketing tactics that might lead to the break-up of a marriage or convince teenagers to be sexually active. But before you jump on this bandwagon, let's review what my role would be in this process. As a marketer, I might encourage television programming that romanticizes extramarital affairs or shows how sexually promiscuous teens live more exciting lives. Why would I do this? Because people who watch this type of programming are more likely to have less stable relationships. And as we established last time, people with less attachment consume more. Ultimately, my job is to sell."

Pressley pulled out her laptop and began taking notes. She knew – knew deeply – that there was a fallacy in his thinking, and she was going to find it. It was like a quest.

"The critic would say I should also include the consequences of such poor choices in my messaging," Maddox said. "Write television scripts about the heartache of the children of divorce or the difficulties that sexually active adolescents have in forming stable relationships later on in life. But guess what? No one is going to watch a show that preaches to them. And I can't sell something if no one is watching. I want eye balls.

"So let parents and preachers speak about morality. I can't be held accountable for parents who no longer engage their children in moral discussion. And neither should you. The smart will learn responsibility and prosper, while the undisciplined will suffer and perish. Darwin was right. Only the fit survive. As Mandeville showed in his 'Fable of the Bees,' there's nobility in making money, even if it comes at someone else's expense.

"Now, who wants to learn how to make money?"

Raucous applause again filled the building.

"Well, then, let's start with the difference between 'self respect' and 'self esteem."

A large image was projected on the screen of a handsome man in a thousand dollar suit juxtaposed against an expressionless farmer in overalls.

"Based only on the appearances of these two men, we might draw a couple of conclusions. We may think the expensively dressed man is successful while the modestly dressed man is poor. This is based on our esteem of both gentlemen. But let's focus on the modest gentleman. His face shows character and strength. We presume he's a hard worker, since farm life is difficult. Farm work is also typically honest since one only reaps what he sows. Also, this man seemingly gives no thought to impressing others – of seeking esteem.

"Do you see the difference? Self esteem is projected on you by others, whereas self respect is internalized and doesn't depend on other people's opinions. Self respect gives no power to others, whereas self esteem seeks constant validation.

"As marketers, it's important to understand that we only have interest in what can be sold. Self respect is therefore of no concern to us. *We* focus on self esteem. We want people who define themselves by products. Social scientists make a distinction between 'ascribed status,' which is unearned, and 'achieved status,' which is based on merit. Our marketing messages ascribe a status to consumers based on their purchasing habits. Think of the aspirational message behind successful marketing campaigns. 'Buy the new Air Jordans and you'll be able to dunk from the free throw line.' 'Purchase the Hemingway bedroom set and your life will be filled with insight, adventure, and distinction.' You all get the picture.

"But I know what you're thinking, what is the historical evolution that allows these marketing messages to be so persuasive?"

The class laughed.

"The concept of self esteem was brought to light in the 1960s by psychologists who believed a person's self-worth was derived by the perceptions of others. Spiritualists had long maintained that each person had an intrinsic value because they were a child of God. They encouraged everyone to nurture this self respect by valuing others and seeking out meaningful work. Spiritualists spoke of an individual's work as their life's mission. Each person's work – regardless of compensation – was noble insofar as it was honest and contributed to a greater whole.

"Self esteem ran counter to these principles. The school of self esteem taught that appearance was more important than achievement. The significance of a person's work was evaluated based upon earnings, not contribution. Therefore, in order to establish value in society, people began to show their wealth, outspending one another trying to impress complete strangers. In the early nineties – for the first time – surveys began to show that young people were more concerned with obtaining and spending wealth than acquiring competency in their profession and contributing to society.

"As our culture grew less religious and individuals lost their sense of self, marketers exploited the opportunity. A person could never look too young, too tan, or too skinny (for example) – regardless of the true measure of that person's health. This gave advertisers considerable sway over consumer preferences. People became hypersensitive over how they conformed to these arbitrary standards and spent money to bridge the gaps.

"Today the idea of self esteem is so ingrained in our culture that no one recognizes the contradiction of indicting a playground bully for calling a classmate fat while exonerating the diet industry for doing the same thing. The only difference is that the bully doesn't make a profit. As marketers, our culture grants us a peculiar license to criticize.

"So how do we use this information to make money? Our objective as marketers is to first identify the types of people who crave societal validation and then to make more of them."

He thought about getting into the moral implications of this practice, if only for another tussle with Pressley. But he'd already made his points. Consumers had the ultimate power in an unfettered free market, and they were free to rebel. It wasn't like he was keeping these practices a secret. He had published his strategies in numerous books and had received little public blowback. The fact that his clients were nuts about the idea ultimately provided all the validation he needed.

"Never in the history of the world have we had the tools at our disposal to identify and capitalize off of profitable consumption patterns so efficiently," Henry said. "Technology allows us to track people's buying preferences in ways we've never imagined. As we analyze these trails of digital bread crumbs, we can segment consumers into distinct categories and customize marketing campaigns specific to their needs. The possibilities of using data to market more effectively are virtually endless."

"Just remember, however, that the digital world has a long memory, and there is no such thing as a secret."

Your gold and silver is cankered;
and the rust of them
shall be a witness against you,
and shall eat your flesh
as it were fire.

- James 5:3 (KJV)

CHAPTER 9

Within a couple of days after Maddox left Zynthe Gaming, Gerald Burke received eleven calls from venture funds inquiring about the cash needs of his company. Within three months Gerald had agreed to accept $250 million for 50 percent of the company. The valuation made Zynthe Gaming worth $500 million. Current revenues were running at only $10 million a year, but the venture fund expected Zynthe to increase revenues to $100 million in one year, $500 million in two years, and to reach revenues of $1 billion annually within three years. In year four, the venture firm would take Zynthe public at ten times revenues, multiplying their $250 million venture investment into $5 billion within three years.

The revenue projections were certainly aggressive but not unprecedented. Gaming companies with similar business models had achieved comparable growth. Gerald felt the pressure, but he was more captivated by the opportunity. He had a 5 percent ownership in the company. If it hit ten billion dollars, he would be worth five hundred million dollars, personally.

Not half bad. And he owed it all to Maddox.

Gerald's executive team arrived to work early and energized – all in the comfort of their new luxury automobiles. Gerald had called a board meeting at seven o'clock in the morning to discuss Zynthe's revised business model in more detail. It had been over six months since Maddox had visited. Zynthe's new data generating games had been tested, launched, and universally well received. The time was right for Gerald to share Maddox's full gaming vision with the executives.

The ten of them were now seated around a state of the art conference room in an office building in tony Palo Alto – Zynthe's new headquarters. Gerald Burke entered the room and reached for a remote control. He pressed a button and electronic curtains retreated into the window frames. Streams of natural light lit up the room. The executives sipped coffee that had been delivered to each of them from Zynthe's personal, onsite Barista.

"You should all have our agenda in front of you," Gerald said, "but before we begin, Irene, how are our employees enjoying their time here at Zynthe?"

"They are enthusiastic and motivated, each and every one of them," Irene, the HR vice president said. "For every available position, we're receiving over one hundred applicants. We're attracting the top technical talent in the world. People can sense that Zynthe represents a unique opportunity."

"And does everyone in this room feel the same?" Gerald asked.

Each person smiled and nodded.

"Good. I think it's important to recognize that throughout history there have only been a handful of companies that have ever come close to the opportunity represented by the Zynthe business model. Our company has transformed almost overnight. You were initially hired to run a much smaller business, so many of you would be considered too young and inexperienced to occupy your job titles in a company of Zynthe's current standing. But Zynthe is on the bleeding edge, and few people have experience in what we're about to do. I'll never blame your inexperience for failure, and I'm not worried about your competency or work ethic. You're all sufficiently hard working and smart enough to confront the challenges that await us. What *does* concern me is your commitment, however. If any of you don't feel comfortable with our revenue model or aggressive growth targets, I need to know now."

Each team member remained locked on Gerald.

"So, you'll remember our meeting with Dr. Henry Maddox about six months ago?"

"Oh yes, in the galaxy far, far, away," Richard Moldt said.

The room responded with silence and blank stares. Chief Operating Officer Sheila Drummond rolled her eyes.

"What? Star Wars. Come on guys. We're a tech company!"

The room laughed. Gerald appreciated the levity.

"In that galaxy far, far, away," Gerald nodded at Richard, "Dr. Maddox suggested some efforts to gather our users' personal data that made some of you feel uncomfortable. Do any of you still feel that way?"

The room was silent.

"I'll take that as a 'no'. I'm glad that you're all still on board. Since that time, I've asked our Chief Technology Officer, Richard Moldt to look into some ways to assure that we're capturing as much user data as possible. Richard?"

All eyes turned to Richard, who didn't bother to stand. "As you recall, I was initially opposed to this idea, but my research has convinced me otherwise. Companies have been doing this throughout the industry. The technology is well established and user resistance has been low. Our gaming model requires that our users create a user login in order to play our games. We tell the user this is important so we can keep track of their progress within the game – the points and credits they've earned. This personalized gaming experience also allows the user to store a credit card on file – enabling any impulse purchases during the game. So we always know exactly who is playing our games and when."

As Moldt was speaking, Gerald walked around the conference table and stood behind him. The gesture was intended to show support for Moldt, though Gerald felt more like an overbearing father not willing to surrender the spotlight to his eager, proud son.

"But" Moldt said, "the game itself is only the first way we'll get user data. We've already talked about how we'll incent users to provide personal information in exchange for credits that can be redeemed within our game or on our partner sites. What we haven't spoken about at length is the tracking software that we'll use. As is the case in many other companies, we'll install cookies on each user's hard drive or smart phone. This tracking software will allow us to expand our data collection outside of the game. This means that if the user decides to visit some websites while still logged into our game, we'll know which ones and how long they stay on each page. Our tracking software will also track the browser activity of each of our users when they're logged out of our game. When the user logs back into the game, the tracking software will upload the data back up to their archived personal data folder on our servers –"

"So essentially we'll have a personal file on each of our users that contains a library of every web page they've ever visited, whether on a computer or a smart phone." Gerald couldn't help stealing the punch line. Maybe he was an overbearing father.

"That's right," Moldt said.

"Sean," Gerald said, "are there any legal problems with this?"

"None to speak of, Gerald," their Chief Council said. "Social networks are currently doing the same thing. As long as we disclose it in our user agreements, we'll be fine."

"Simon, is there anything from an information gathering perspective you want to add?"

"Only that we have the ability to not only link all of the data with a person but also to their handheld smart phone," their Chief Mobil Officer said. "Each smart phone has a GPS locater so we can track where our users are at any given point in time."

"David, tell us how you'll keep users playing our game."

"Okay, this is cool," David, their Chief Product Officer said. "More than any other gaming experience, it's important that 'freemium' games suck the user in. We want the user to escape from reality into a world where they have more control than they can ever have in everyday life. As the user's proficiency in the game improves, they get more stuff, which gives them a sense of achievement. They can play with others who are also online, which will provide a sense of sociability. As the user gains more gaming rewards, the user will start to get prestige amongst their online peers. We'll have some rewards that can only be achieved as a team, so we'll use peer pressure to keep users within the game because they won't want to let down their other virtual team members. Online users will rely on each other, which will give them a sense of purpose. The whole point is to make the user experience not just enjoyable but habit forming."

Gerald was now looking out the windows of the conference room. He squinted at the not too distant Hoover Tower on Stanford University's adjacent campus as it came into focus. Zynthe's vision was finally becoming clear, refined. There was just one more piece.

"Blaire? How do we turn this into money?"

"Based on what Richard and Simon described," the Chief Marketing Officer said, "you can begin to see the types of information we'll gather. We'll monetize this data through four important ways: 1) gaming revenue, 2) advertising, 3) marketing lists, and 4) partner referrals. Once the user has played our free version of the game a few times, we'll begin to offer them low dollar upgrades – they can change their avatar character's hair color or clothing for a dollar, for example. Once the user begins to participate in the low dollar upgrades, we'll sell them on higher priced promotions. We've established an entire array of menu options that include everything from purchasing an online pet to decorating your online house. We'll even have special promotions that will run on holidays, where they can change the theme of the game to a Christmas, Valentine's Day, or Independence Day theme for example – for a cost.

"But our gaming revenue is minor compared to the advertising revenue. Our pay per click and pay per impression advertising will allow companies to target specific consumer segments with a laser-like focus. Companies will be amazed at the return on their investment as we narrow the exact profile of the user who's actually buying their products. Sometimes the data can be very surprising, which makes it that much more valuable.

"For companies that want to market outside of our game, we can sell marketing lists – of say, single females who visit entertainment websites for more than six hours each week, live in Arizona, make over $50 thousand a year, and commute at least an hour each way to work. The specificity of our users' demographic information will be unparalleled.

"Then there are the partner referrals. Whether it's through the gaming experience or as a promotion, we'll grant our users credits to be used with our partners, with whom we've negotiated a commission structure."

"Thank you Blaire," Gerald said. "This is all very exciting. But I wanted to say a word about these partner referrals."

Gerald turned away from the window, walked over, and closed the conference room door. He then resumed his seat at the head of the table.

"I've recently spent some time negotiating with some possible partners," Gerald said. "All of these companies are very excited about the potential our platform will provide them to expand their business. In particular I've been negotiating with some forms of adult entertainment."

Gerald took a long sip from his coffee. No serious reaction yet.

"More specifically, I have been speaking with online gambling and pornography websites."

He could see resistance beginning to build, but he pressed on before it could take hold.

"Now at first blush, I know some of you may object to this direction. Let me assure you that Zynthe Gaming will not develop content for these types of businesses. We'll always keep an arm's length relationship between us and them. For instance, these revenues will only be disclosed on our financial statements as 'partner referral' revenues, so at no time will any of your neighbors, church members, PTA associates, or family members ever accuse you of working in these industries.

"The truth of the matter is that in order to compete in the online world, you need to tap into these types of revenue streams. The data is clear, if a person spends a significant amount of time on the internet, they'll eventually end up viewing and then paying for access to pornography. This same user profile will also gamble in online casinos. The data shows that our users would be highly likely to spend money on these adult entertainment sites. If we don't refer them, they would probably end up there any way. Why not profit off of an introduction?"

Gerald's pitch was sixth months in the making. He delivered it as he had rehearsed, with little emotion. The executives needed to understand that this was just another cost of doing business.

Tad Lee adjusted his chair and cleared his throat. "I don't like this direction, not one bit. But I'm not naive, however. Gerald is right. Our users would find these sites without us, so why not get a cut? I used to work in the hotel industry, and pay per view pornography was provided in all of the hotel rooms – in hotel chains that had ethical, moral, and often times very religious people on their boards. This is no different. I don't think we need to feel hesitant about this in the least."

"As long as we only refer adults, I'm fine with it," Sheila Drummond said.

"To be clear, we'll refer everyone," said Gerald. "The destination website will be in charge of verifying their age. This way we can't be held responsible if an underage user somehow goes undetected when they hop from our environment to theirs."

"Okay. But we'll be following industry standards?" Sheila said.

"Absolutely."

"It certainly isn't illegal," Sean Larson said.

"Look," Gerald said, "I want your entire commitment. I don't want anyone to cause me any problems down the line on this. Is there any one in here who objects?"

Gerald Burke looked at each executive individually. Each person shook their head.

"Okay then," Gerald said. "We're all good. Now my last question is for Richard. And I want a straight answer. How fast have you gotten up to in your AMG SLS Roadster?"

Ear to ear smiles filled the room.

But I've drawn the conclusion,
it's all an illusion
Confusion's the name of the game
A misconception,
a vast deception,
Something got to change

- India Arie, "Video" (2002)

CHAPTER 10

Laroy and his wife Margaret were having dinner at their modest home, in the East Bay community of Pleasanton.

"Laroy, why are you so quiet?"

Laroy came out of his reverie and looked at his plate. He'd hardly touched his dinner but didn't feel at all hungry. "I don't know what to do Margaret. I feel like I understand the problems, but I can't find solutions."

"Are you still thinking about your visit to New Beginnings? Ben and internet addiction?"

"Internet addiction's just the latest. Companies have been profiting off of the suffering of others since beer companies offered free lunches in bars. Historically, our response has been to launch information campaigns, to educate people on the dangers. But mostly we only get to people after they've been hurt, and with the mass media and the internet, they're getting hurt faster, and we're falling farther and farther behind. I wish there was some way to get out in front of this.

"We're losing the youth because even though we know *what* to tell them, we don't know *how* to talk to them. Young people stopped using email and switched to Facebook. So we mounted an ad campaign on Facebook only to find they only respond to texts. Once we developed a text strategy, they'd gone to Tweets. We can't keep up because what's driving the development of these new forms of communication is exactly what we're trying to fight against."

"Which is?"

"Manipulation!" Laroy took a deep breath. No need to yell at Margaret over this. It wasn't her fault. "These new media companies have the same motivations as the old media companies. They exist to sell products and services. The difference is that traditional media used to speak to broad demographics – teenagers, suburban fathers, urban singles. The new media companies can now target a person by name. They know each person's specific preferences, habits, and weaknesses. They can tailor a message so convincing that even the disciplined and educated can't resist."

"Isn't there some historical model for how to deal with this?"

"How can you apply an historical model when all of this technology is unprecedented?"

Margaret sat back in her chair. Her hair was shiny and silver, cut in a bob, which fit both her age and young energy.

"Well, history does teach that technology breakthroughs intended for even the crudest of purposes can be used for the most worthy of causes."

"What do you have in mind?"

"The Roman road network. Fifty thousand miles of paved roads built to move troops and allow generals to communicate. And yet they allowed trade and travel that kept the Empire together."

"Now you're just showing off."

"Maybe a little bit." Margaret shot Laroy a flirtatious grin. "The Pax Romana lasted for two centuries because of this road network. And during the 'Pax Romana', Roman rule expanded to cover about two million square miles."

"Okay," Laroy said, "so what do Roman roads have to do with modern day marketing gimmicks?"

"Ah, and here's the connection dear husband. These same roads that were used for the often brutal benefit of the Romans were also used in an unintended, significant, historic, and virtuous way. The Apostle Paul was converted on one of those roads – the road to Damascus – and then spent the next few decades using those roads to spread Christianity throughout the Empire.

"Paul was familiar with the Roman road networks because he was a Roman Citizen; he traveled freely among the provinces. You need to find someone, like Paul, who is familiar with the digital infrastructure of today. Equally as important, you need someone, like Paul, who's acquainted with the strategies of the opposition.

"Laroy, you need a convert."

You cannot make men good by law:
and without good men
you cannot have a good society.

- C.S. Lewis, "Mere Christianity"

CHAPTER 11

The building was pleasant but nondescript. Four stories of poured concrete and smoked glass with an occasional stringcourse of brick so the architect could justify earning his wage. Immature plantings out front would eventually grow into uninspiring landscaping. No corporate signage. Henry double checked the address in his iPhone. This was the place. He entered the small lobby and approached the receptionist. She was seated behind a counter that looked like it was purchased in one piece, as a floor model at Ikea.

"Pardon me; I'm looking for the offices of SOF, Inc. Do you know where I might find them?"

"One second, please." The receptionist scanned a registry.

"Take your time, I'm a little early." Henry smiled. "I'm relieved to know that I'm not the only one having a hard time finding them."

"I'm sorry for the delay," the receptionist said. "You see, we lease office spaces and conference rooms by the day.

So it's hard to keep up with all of the different companies that come through here."

"I understand." It was odd, though. What kind of company didn't even have its own conference space? Were they out of state? "So it sounds like you know as little about the company as I do."

"Or less. The only thing I know about SOF is that they reserved our small conference room today from nine to five. Just go down this hallway and take your first right. The conference room is number 104. It will be on your left. You can wait there until the rest of your party arrives."

"Thank you."

Henry entered the conference room and sat down at a table that would maybe hold eight people. He was five minutes early. Before he came, he'd scoured the internet to learn about SOF, Inc. but found nothing. He had received the consultation request through his website. The only reason he even came to the appointment was because SOF had prepaid his ten thousand dollar retainer. That at least meant they weren't a hoax.

At times, Henry's clients preferred to use an alias to remain anonymous. He always honored such requests. SOF had not mentioned anonymity, but that may have simply been an oversight. In any case, even anonymous clients would eventually tell him why they wanted to hire him.

Though he would have preferred to know ahead of time what he was getting into. That way he could prepare. Now . . . he would need to be nimble. He had data from enough different industries on his laptop to provide a week's worth of insights. He could certainly satisfy SOF for eight hours.

As Henry typed in the password into his computer, he heard the door knob turn. Henry stood, composed himself, and approached the door.

As the door opened, an older gentleman entered the room. The man possessed neither the brashness of a tech executive nor the elegance of a Fortune 500 business leader.

The man extended his hand and with a warm, confident voice said, "Dr. Maddox, my name is Laroy Elden it's nice to finally meet you."

Woe unto them
that call evil good,
and good evil;
that put darkness for light,
and light for darkness;
that put bitter for sweet,
and sweet for bitter!

- Isaiah 5:20 (KJV)

CHAPTER 12

"Have a seat Mr. Elden."

"Thank you, Dr. Maddox."

"Henry, please."

Laroy studied Maddox as he settled back into his seat. He had watched a number of his presentations online, and the man in person seemed to exhibit the same sort of energy and charm as he did on the small screen. His clothes were expensive but understated, aimed to impress the cognoscenti while leaving everyone else at ease. And he showed an open, almost endearing curiosity. Assuming it was genuine, of course.

"I must admit that you have the advantage of me," Maddox said. "You know something about my consultancy but I know nothing about you."

"I apologize for the sketchiness of my request, Henry. I felt it best to keep my business confidential. In that same vein, do you mind if I ask you some questions before we proceed?"

"Ask away, Mr. Elden."

"Do you have any children?"

"No sir."

"Are you married?"

"Not at the present."

"Do you consider family important?"

"Mr. Elden, I find this course of questioning very personal."

"I apologize. I don't mean to make you feel uncomfortable." Laroy adjusted his posture and cleared his throat. "Henry, I got married when I was twenty two years old. I don't know if anyone gets married that young anymore. My wife and I raised four children together. My oldest daughter passed away over twenty years ago. She died too soon. She was only eighteen."

"I'm sorry to hear that."

"She died of heart failure."

"That young? Life can be unfair."

"It certainly can. In Jenny's case, the problem could've been prevented though. You see, the heart failure was caused by an eating disorder. A couple of years before she started to compare her body with the models, dancers, pop stars, and actresses promoted in the media. Gossip columns hounded these famous women for gaining as few as a couple of pounds. Jenny heard those same critical voices when she looked in the mirror. My daughter, who had once been outgoing, gifted, and kind, became reclusive and critical. We sent her to nutritionists, counselors, and camps. We surrounded her with people who loved her. It wasn't enough. I blame irresponsible advertisers for her death."

Henry leaned forward towards Laroy. "I'm sorry for your loss Mr. Elden."

"Making a marriage work and raising children have been the most challenging responsibilities of my life. I think that, in recent years, it's gotten even harder. It's as if our culture doesn't want to see families succeed anymore."

Maddox said nothing, but still seemed politely interested.

"I have to admit when I first got married, I did it out of convention," Laroy said. "That was what people did when I was young. And no sooner did you get married than you were expected to have children. Before I knew it, I was a young father trying to figure out how to support a wife and four kids. It was often overwhelming, but I did the best I could. I certainly have regrets about the way I parented, but I never regret having been a father. It's made me a better person. I'm more patient, selfless, loving, and committed than I otherwise would have been. I think life is less about acquisition than it is about refinement. That is the secret to joy."

"You seem like a wise person Mr. Elden."

"I've paid the price for it. A price too few people are willing to pay these days."

Laroy reached for a bottle of water from the middle of the conference room table, twisted the cap and took a drink.

He then slid another bottle over to Henry. "I paid for these. We might as well make use of them."

With a nod, Henry caught the bottle.

"I now have nine grandchildren. It's interesting how being a grandparent changes your perspective of life. I worry constantly about my grandchildren and the world they'll inherit."

Laroy took another sip of his water.

"Henry do you know what it means to be provincial?"

"Well, typically that term is used to describe a lack of sophistication. I suppose it originated based on the way citizens of small provinces behaved when they entered larger, more diverse cities."

"That's the traditional definition. In addition to having a regional application, however, I believe that provincialism applies across time as well. You see, people who grow up in one time period sometimes feel the traditions of former generations no longer apply to them. I think this type of thinking is provincial."

Maddox fidgeted in his chair, the first sign of genuine emotion Laroy had seen.

"I contrast provincialism with the transcendent – the thought that certain customs or traditions transcend time and regions. It's at our own peril that we allow our culture to discard transcendent customs. The traditions of marriage and raising children are (in my mind) transcendent. The world today views these customs as provincial . . . that in some way we've outgrown the need for them. This concerns me a great deal."

"Mr. Elden, I apologize for interrupting and I don't mean to be impolite, but I just want to make sure you understand that you are paying for my time right now. Does this course of discussion have anything to do with how I can help your business?"

Laroy turned and looked Henry in the eyes. "Dr. Maddox, my business is *you*. Your strategies are destroying families."

Maddox raised one hand to stroke the back of his neck. "Mr. Elden, you seem like a very sincere man. But with all due respect, I feel very comfortable with my chosen profession."

"Henry, the family has historically been the fundamental unit of society. Destroy that, and you won't have a society to support your chosen profession."

Maddox shook his head slowly. "I'm sorry, your premise is flawed. I don't destroy families. Families destroy themselves."

"You manipulate consumers by feeding on their ignorance. You encourage reckless spending for worthless items."

"According to free market principles, every product is worth what people pay for it. But did you invite me here . . ." Henry stopped and then restarted. "Are you paying me 1,200 dollars an hour to listen to a sermon? If so, there are more effective ways to spend your money. Every profamily organization on the planet has lobbed these same arguments at me . . . for years. Do you think I'm going to suddenly come around to your point of view?"

"My hope is that the timing and urgency of my request might cause you to rethink some things."

"I've actually spent much of my life thinking about these things. My perspective is pretty clear. I don't see that protecting consumers from themselves is my responsibility."

Laroy paused to catch his breath. How to defuse the tension?

"Henry, when I was young, my hero was the Lone Ranger. I used to listen to the series on the radio – we didn't have a television in my home until I was in high school. That was probably my first introduction to what we now call media. The Lone Ranger made quite an impression on me. He adhered to a strict moral code. I still find myself echoing some of his refrains, like 'that all things change but truth, and that truth alone, live on forever' or '...that sooner or later . . . somewhere . . . somehow . . . we must settle with the world and make payment for what we have taken.' I've forgotten much but somehow, I can still vividly recall Lone Ranger episodes from the fifties.

"Since the passing of my daughter Jenny I've thought a lot about the influence of media on our culture. I think one of the problems is that technology distances the purveyors of media from their consumers. They don't see the effect that their programming has on individuals, families. They only see their profits. Historically, communication was more intimate. I think the lack of proximity dulls conscience.

"Henry, I respectfully ask you to rethink your marketing tactics. You're right. I owe you an explanation for calling you here to meet with me today. SOF, Inc. stands for Save Our Families. It's a not-for-profit corporation I created after my daughter died. I believe that modern media messaging is damaging children. And the frustrating thing is that most people agree with me. But no one cares. I can't motivate people to act. The pitchmen for pro-family causes have been discredited, maligned, and compartmentalized. Too many pro-family advocates have been disgraced because their actions don't match their rhetoric. Some of the great pro-family arguments set forth by religious minds are dismissed because the messengers' opinions are informed by faith, and we are living in an increasingly irreligious society. Other advocates continue to preach to the choir, but they can't expand their reach. We especially need to find a better way of reaching young people. The coveted 18 to 34 year-old advertising demographic (to use your language) has been lost to popular culture and consumerism. We need a messenger who can speak their language, communicate with them on their terms and in their way. And that's why I asked you here.

"I want to hire you to fight for the family."

Maddox simply stared for a moment, holding his friendly-consultant smile. Then he began to chuckle.

"You're serious? You understand the conflict that this would cause with my other clients? I would be attacking the institutions and structures I have built up. And I would almost certainly be fired. Would you compensate me for all of that lost revenue?"

"Henry, can't you see that your current strategies are unsustainable, not to mention immoral? They work for short term gain but the profits come at too steep a price. I'm asking you to join with me in supporting families, communities . . . out of the goodness of your heart."

"Remarkable," Maddox said. "I don't know if I should admire your audacity or fear your naiveté. Even if people did listen and respond to your message, powerful corporate interests would ramp up another propaganda campaign. Do you have the financial resources to go toe-to-toe with corporate America?" Maddox stood up. "I'm sorry, but you couldn't pay me enough to join your cause, Mr. Elden. I'm afraid you've wasted both your and my time this morning. Have a good day sir."

Laroy approached Maddox and shook his hand. Then, with a final smile and nod, Maddox turned and left.

Laroy collapsed back into his seat. He had given Maddox his best shot. So where was the miracle?

...and the day that cometh
shall burn them up,
saith the Lord of hosts,
that it shall leave them
neither root nor branch.

- Malachi 4:1 (KJV)

CHAPTER 13

Henry drove far too fast straight from that bizarre meeting with Laroy Elden to his own offices in the East Bay. The smoked glass on the front doors rattled as he burst into his office.

"Henry what's wrong?"

"Cheryl, I just wasted my whole morning with an old man who lectured me on how my philosophies break apart the family. That I was destroying society."

"This was your appointment with SOF, Inc.?"

"Yes."

"You mean he paid a ten thousand dollar deposit to spend an hour lecturing you?"

"Well, not exactly. He wanted to hire me to fight for his cause."

"And what is his cause?"

"He's in the family business."

"So what's his family's business? Does his family run a funeral home or something?"

"No. His business is the family."

"I don't understand."

"Sorry. I'm a little flustered. Let me slow down." Henry took a deep breath. "SOF, Inc. stands for Save Our Families. It's a small nonprofit that advocates against antifamily forces. I told him that it would not be in my best interest to accept him as a client."

"To say the least. I can imagine what all of our clients would say if you began fighting on behalf of profamily causes."

"Yeah, it wouldn't go over well. Look, Cheryl, I want you to reverse the ten thousand dollar charge on SOF, Inc.'s credit card. I don't feel good about collecting money for this."

Cheryl grinned. "I bet it feels good to take the moral high ground with a profamily organization, eh?"

Henry laughed. "Ah, how well you know me."

"What made this man think that you of all people could be persuaded to fight for the family, Henry?"

"I don't know. He had certainly done his homework. He must have known that stopping me would do very little to advance his cause. There are plenty of other people like me who would just take my place."

"He probably wanted to start at the top and work his way down."

"Perhaps . . ."

"I can't imagine him getting a better reception from the likes of Jeff Hoffman or Harmony Winter."

Hang on, though. Now that Henry was calming down, he was beginning to think again. "But what if they did take up his cause? It would change the entire landscape of what we're doing."

"What do you mean?"

"You remember my lecture on self esteem vs. self respect?"

"I put together your slides. Self esteem is defined by products, bestowed by the market, not earned. Self respect is earned and internalized. People with self respect don't give power to others. Yeah, great lecture."

"And you remember that, as marketers, we spend our time on those seeking self esteem because they can be influenced. We don't waste our efforts on those who have self respect."

"So what's your point?"

"Profamily advocates are typically more driven by faith than other groups, right?"

"I'd guess so, sure."

"Remember the part of my lecture where I observed that people of faith felt that their identity came from their spirituality and not by their consumption?"

"Yeah . . ."

"Well representing SOF, Inc. would be an extraordinary experiment. What if we could gather the type of data we normally collect on a group who is among the most spiritually motivated and least inclined to frivolous consumption? We just might be able to crack the code on how to fragment a hugely untapped market. This would be virgin territory. We would have absolutely no competition. This could be the holy grail of advertising."

"Henry, are you suggesting you accept SOF, Inc. as a client for the sole purpose of exploiting their members?"

"Better us than Hoffman or Winter. This will help to remind my former students that I'm still the teacher. Do you have any contact information for Laroy Elden?"

"I can look on SOF, Inc.'s consultancy request. There should be a phone number on there."

"Good. Call Mr. Elden and tell him that I'll accept his offer. Tell him I won't charge him any money, but in order to be effective I do need to retain ownership of all of the data we accumulate in advancing his cause. And then tell him I want to meet with him as soon as possible to get started."

"And what should I tell him caused you to change your mind?"

"Just tell him I had a change of heart. Those spiritual types love that sort of thing."

"Thank you for meeting me here Dr. Maddox. I was overjoyed to get your call. I'd already committed to volunteer here at New Beginnings, and I felt this would be the perfect way to familiarize you to our cause."

"Mr. Elden, I want to apologize if I was rude to you yesterday. It wasn't until I got back to my office that I realized the type of opportunity that working with SOF would provide. And please, call me Henry."

"Very well Henry. Call me Laroy."

Laroy led Henry into the New Beginnings' warm, living-room-like lobby, where Jennifer Bennett was waiting for them.

"Jennifer, I want you to meet a business associate and friend of mine," he said. "This is Henry Maddox. Henry, Jennifer is the facility manager here at New Beginnings."

"Nice to meet you Henry. I take it Laroy's explained a bit about what we do here?"

"Actually, very little. I think he wanted to surprise me. So I'd appreciate a brief introduction."

"Well, New Beginnings was formed five years ago to address the growing problem of internet addiction. An internet addiction is any behavior that causes people to prefer living in a digital world to the real world – online shopping, social networking, endlessly surfing the internet, gaming, online gambling, and online pornography. These types of addictions distance people from the people they once loved. They also rob individuals of their dignity as productive citizens within their communities. Families often turn to us as a last resort."

"Correct me if I'm wrong Mrs. Bennett," Henry said, "but isn't 'addiction' a medical term?"

"Yes, you're right. And the use of the term has come under scrutiny from some organizations because it hasn't been officially accepted as a clinical diagnosis. We base our use of the term on the emerging notion that all addiction can be defined in terms of changes to the brain rather than specific causes. It's a definition that has recently been embraced by the American Society of Addiction Medicine. There's irrefutable evidence that those people who spend unhealthy amounts of time on the internet do so because of the way the digital stimuli manipulate the rewards center of the brain. We think it's just a matter of time before the Diagnostic and Statistical Manual of Mental Disorders recognizes internet addiction as a clinical disorder."

"It looks like this whole emerging digital addiction has created quite the market opportunity for a place like New Beginnings," Henry said.

"We're certainly busy, which I guess is a good and a bad thing," said Jennifer.

"I don't mean to be cynical Mrs. Bennett but this is quite a business. How can you be conflicted at the success of your facility?"

"It's true we developed this facility to serve a market need. But you can't spend a day here, seeing the pain our patients and their families experience, and somehow take pleasure in earning a good paycheck. Besides, I could use my schooling and experience to make much more money somewhere else. I look at my work here as much more of a calling than a job."

"Well, I applaud you Jennifer," Laroy said. "Our world would certainly be a better place if more people had motives like you. Don't you think Henry?"

"Absolutely."

"Well, let's not overdo it. I'm blessed to do something where I feel I can make a difference."

"Jennifer," Laroy said, "I believe I'm scheduled to check in with Benjamin, is that correct?"

"He's waiting. I think you'll be pleased at his progress."

"Is there someone with whom Henry could visit?"

"I'm sorry but since Mr. Maddox hasn't undergone our orientation, I can't have him interact directly with our patients. I can only have him observe from a distance."

"That's fine," Henry said.

"Okay, I'll go see if Benjamin is ready."

Jennifer walked down the facility's corridor, leaving Henry and Laroy alone.

"Henry, you're an interesting study," Laroy said.

"How so?"

"It almost sounded like you thought New Beginnings should somehow be grateful that internet addiction has grown to be such a pervasive problem."

"You have to admit, New Beginnings has an interest in exaggerating the extent of this so called digital addiction. I don't fault them. In fact, they're doing exactly what I teach my clients. Most businesses find their markets, smart businesses create them."

Henry walked over to a six foot wide by three foot tall fish tank in the reception area. He tapped on the aquarium's glass to attract the attention of a passing puffer fish. "Yes, I actually read some of your books before meeting with you yesterday," Laroy said. "You embrace Mandeville's idea that private vices lead to a public benefit. But have you considered Frederic Bastiat's 'Parable of the Broken Window.'"

"Superficially. How do you understand Bastiat?"

"As you may know, Bastiat lived in early nineteenth century France. He was a fierce advocate for free markets, but he came to a much different conclusion than you or

Mandeville." Laroy joined Henry at the fish tank. "The Parable of the Broken Window speaks of a shopkeeper whose son carelessly breaks a pane of glass. "Observers of the event consoled the shop keeper by saying, 'It is an ill wind that blows nobody good. Everybody must live, and what would become of the glaziers if panes of glass were never broken?'"

"That would be my point."

"Right, destruction is good because it employs people. Bastiat, however, refuted this notion. He's the first theorist to explore the concept of 'opportunity cost.' Bastiat admitted that the glazier was enriched by the cost of replacing the window, which he put at six francs. He called this event, 'that which was seen.' But there was another part of the equation, 'that which was unseen – the opportunity cost of those six francs. If the shopkeeper didn't spend his six francs on repairing the window, he could have spent them on, say, new shoes. Instead of enriching the glazier, the shopkeeper would have enriched the shoemaker and the shopkeeper would have received a useful product in return. The broken window therefore harmed two people, the shopkeeper and the shoemaker, while only benefiting one, the glazier. In Bastiat's own words –" Laroy closed his eyes, calling to mind the strange rhythms of the nineteenth century translation. "'Society loses the value of things which are uselessly destroyed . . . to break, to spoil, to waste, is not to encourage national labor; or, more briefly, 'destruction is not profit.'"

"Dr. Maddox, there's your first lesson of the day. Destruction ultimately benefits no one. True, a facility like

New Beginnings exists because of a destructive market need. But if resources weren't expended on repairing damage, they could have been employed in something much more productive. That's why I think your approach ultimately threatens capitalism."

Maddox freed himself from the allure of the fish tank long enough to acknowledge Laroy's point, though Laroy got the feeling it was more politeness than conviction.

Within a couple of minutes, Jennifer Bennett appeared in the reception area and motioned for the gentlemen to follow her. She escorted Henry to a visitor's room overlooking the facility. The viewpoint allowed Henry to observe different patients, all involved in various activities. All of the patients were young men – there must have been another facility dedicated to women and older men. One young man was practicing the acoustic guitar, another was reading, and another was painting. He saw Laroy greet a young man and then sit down in a conversational area.

Laroy looked interested in what the young man had to say but it was obvious that the flow of conversation was all in one direction. Laroy's words were followed by long periods of silence. Man, talk about dodging a bullet – an awkward conversation with a moody teenager, no thanks.

If Laroy found Henry to be an interesting study, Henry was equally fascinated by Laroy. Laroy was obviously dedicated and sincere. In fact, none of this activity was motivated by financial gain. It was a puzzle. How do you motivate a man (and his followers) to provide you with their intimate personal data when they're not motivated by consumption? A man like Laroy Elden would never waste time on a social network playing video games. Neither would he consume to the point where his purchases would reveal any useful data patterns.

Henry fixated on Laroy's gestures as he interacted with the patient. Laroy demonstrated sincere emotion at the smallest of acknowledgments from the young man.

People like Laroy become passionate about causes, not consumption. What if he were to create a campaign that united all the procommunity forces together in one? The cause would be the key to extracting personal information about each of the campaign's participants. The data could be used to research trends that could help identify, nurture, and then fragment the group's consumption needs.

Henry picked up his cell phone and dialed Cheryl.

"Cheryl, setup a campaign launch for next week at the University. We want to make a big splash – all the bells and whistles. The name of the campaign? We'll call it . . . 'Destruction is Not Profit.'"

Without promotion
something terrible happens...
Nothing!

- PT Barnum

CHAPTER 14

One Week Later

Television news trucks surrounded the campus auditorium. Students not enrolled in Maddox's class assembled to find the source of the commotion until the crowd outside of the building swelled to over five hundred people . . . and continued to grow.

Henry and Laroy were backstage discussing strategy. At the university's request, the students had arrived an hour early to take their seats. The roar of the crowd was loud enough that Henry had to shout.

"All of the major media outlets are here. Remember, don't just pay attention to the big cameras carrying the network logos. Be respectful of the smaller cell phone cameras as well. Video clips will be uploaded to YouTube as well as popular and niche blogs, and you don't want to pull a Michelle Bachmann, apparently staring into space because you're looking at the wrong camera."

"Should we go over our lines one more time?"

"No, we don't want to make this look too stiff. Be yourself. You know the talking points. Don't get too concerned if I go off script for a while. Sometimes I like to riff."

"Riff? I thought we were going to stay on point?"

"Yeah, well I do better when I keep it loose."

Laroy took a deep breath. "Just don't leave me stranded out there. I'm not used to this type of circus atmosphere."

"If you get in trouble, just defer to me, okay?"

"Okay."

"Listen, you wanted exposure for your cause. This is what it looks like. Let's not mess this up."

Henry motioned to Laroy to follow him to the side of the stage. The music that was playing quieted. The President of the University walked to the center of the stage and began the introductions.

"A week ago, I received a call from Professor Maddox. He told me that he and a representative of a profamily organization called Save Our Families had started to work together. Professor Maddox asked if they could use our auditorium to make a major announcement.

"Now to put this in perspective, you must understand that I receive several letters a week from profamily proponents, asking me to terminate Professor Maddox's employment. So when I heard that Professor Maddox and Save Our Families were working together, I double checked my caller ID. I then worried that someone had stolen his cell phone and was impersonating him."

Polite laughter filled the auditorium. Henry leaned toward Laroy. "You know, he agreed to do this to shut my critics up."

"Students in this room of course know Professor Maddox well," the President said. "He needs no welcome or introduction. I do, however, feel obliged to introduce Professor Maddox's co-presenter. Laroy Elden has been President of Save Our Families for over two decades. Save Our Families has partnered with some of the largest profamily organizations in the nation to advance common causes. He's been married for forty years and has four children. His eldest child passed away twenty years ago, when she was only eighteen years-old of complications related to an eating disorder. This daughter, Jenny, serves as the inspiration for Mr. Elden's procommunity involvement. Mr. Elden has nine grandchildren and currently resides in nearby Pleasanton, California.

"So ladies and gentlemen, please provide a warm welcome for Professor Henry Maddox and his guest Mr. Laroy Elden."

Henry strutted on stage with the bravado of a bull fighter. Laroy followed, content to let Henry attract the attention and bask in the applause. The stage had been set-up to mimic the living room of a home. Two comfortable red chairs occupied center stage while a fake, wallpapered wall with a window and family photographs stood behind them.

Laroy's wireless microphone squealed as he sat down. Not wanting to recline too far into the overstuffed cushions, Laroy moved forward to balance himself on the edge of his chair. He hoped he looked eager and engaged. He felt wooden.

Henry flopped into his chair as if he had just arrived home after a long day at work. "Thank you for allowing us to speak with you today," said Henry. "My class is, of course, used to my antics, but I want to welcome all of the media outlets to our classroom. Apparently, having me appear in the same room as a profamily advocate is newsworthy. Don't worry, I haven't gone soft on you."

Henry leaned forward, making it look a lot more natural than Laroy had managed. "Laroy Elden approached me a little over a week ago with a bold idea. Upset at what he felt my strategies were doing to weaken the structure of the family, he asked to hire me. Now, I'm not above being bought, but I'm certainly not a cheap date."

Henry waited for the modest laughter to subside.

"Over the ensuing days, Laroy and I worked out an arrangement. I'm still representing my existing clients, but I'm also representing him. To the casual observer, you may think that this causes a conflict. Indeed, in most cases it does. But as you know, I'm a capitalist. I go where my bread is buttered. And so Laroy and I have embarked on an experiment of sorts. Laroy would you like to explain to these good people why we're here?"

"Yes, thank you Henry." Laroy adjusted his wireless microphone. "Ladies and gentlemen I believe Professor Maddox's market fragmentation strategies are in direct opposition to the idea of community. Communities thrive when people are concerned for one another. Our current digital world encourages isolation and incivility. Digital message boards are filled with venom. We're losing the compassion and empathy that have made our culture great.

"As digital consumers of information, we've placed ourselves in silos that prevent us from communicating with people of other belief systems. This isn't healthy for us individually, nor does it contribute to a better society. There is much common ground where most people can agree. I want to bring people together, not break them apart. Unfortunately many corporations are profiting on this ignorance and division.

"I think if consumers are informed, this knowledge will lead them to purchase goods and services that support communities, not destroy them. I advocate a form of capitalism that encourages social responsibility and strengthens morality, where businesses create a net benefit not just a corporate profit. I think we can accomplish this ideal through information sharing and transparency – not coercion and regulation. We're going to prove that virtue and self-interest can coexist.

"Ladies and gentlemen, I'm pleased to introduce the information hub of our effort . . . henrymaddox.com!"

Henry and Laroy arose from their chairs. In an instant, the fake living room wall and chairs were pulled into the wings and a gigantic screen unraveled from the ceiling. An enormous image of henrymaddox.com's homepage appeared on the screen.

"One of my conditions of employment was that we use my brand for this effort," said Henry. "If this effort fails, it's because of Laroy. If it succeeds it's because of me."

Dispersed laughter again filled the room.

"I do appreciate Henry's willingness to lend his brand to this effort," said Laroy. "We can only conduct this experiment with the integration of the most current technologies and media. Henry lends credibility to the cause in this regard."

Laroy reached in his pocket, pulled out a laser pointer, and directed it at the screen.

"The objective of henrymaddox.com is to organize, educate, and motivate concerned citizens in improving our communities through applying free market principles. In today's consumer driven culture, we vote with our dollars. Henrymaddox.com asks you to think about every dollar you spend and how it shapes our culture.

"The henrymaddox.com home page will highlight an array of different companies. We'll feature companies that are honest, that provide a valuable product or service to the consumer, and that are socially responsible. We'll ask you to support these companies. Our hope is that we can increase sales for the good businesses to the point that other companies will take notice and adopt admirable business practices as well.

"On the opposite end of the spectrum, many massive corporations now have very little to no legitimate competition. Some of these corporations have even become 'too big to fail.' Even the shareholders of these enterprises are so numerous and fragmented that they have no collective voice. Long gone are the days that an owner of a business felt a responsibility to his community and his customers. No wonder the legal name for corporation in Spanish is 'sociedad anónima' – anonymous society.

"So, in addition to spotlighting good companies, we'll also expose companies that are sneaky and destructive. Capitalism is about having choices. Henrymaddox.com is going to give you a voice – both individually and collectively. Get ready, because we're going to make a difference!"

"I think this is as animated as I've ever seen Laroy," Henry said. "I'd sign up just to not disappoint him. Let me quickly call your attention to a couple of other features to our website and our campaign. As you can see, we have a tab where you can sign-up to receive daily emails. You can 'follow' us on Twitter and 'like us' on Facebook. We want you to register with us and provide us with as much information as possible so we can interact with more people like you. We want an army of fellow advocates ready to respond to calls for action when we send out alerts.

"In the upper right hand corner of the website, you can see a counter of how many followers have registered so far. As this number gets larger, we'll have more collective influence in convincing businesses to reform bad business practices.

"Now as a disclaimer, I want to emphasize that my role in this exercise is as a consultant. I'm being paid to execute Laroy's vision. I will not be the one who chooses which companies to target or any of the details of the specific campaigns. You all personally know my feelings as to the role of capitalism – it's inherently amoral. Good businesses identify and respond to markets. Smart businesses create their own markets. If Laroy's efforts are successful, he will have created a significant and untapped market potential. And that's something I can get behind."

Henry looked back at Laroy who indicated he wanted one last word.

"For too long now," said Laroy, "corporations have had access to our personal information without returning the favor. They know everything about us. We know very little about them. This all changes today. Technology can either contribute to an open society that increases consumer leverage or it can be used to exploit and destroy individuals and communities. You now have an opportunity to decide the type of world you want to live in. Please register on henrymaddox.com to start fighting."

Henry looked at Laroy and nodded in approval.

"We'll be available to the press for a limited time for questions," said Henry. "Otherwise, thank you for coming."

The audience's applause was quickly drowned out by the resuming music blaring through the sound system. Students exited into pandemonium outside of the auditorium. Spectators now numbered into the thousands. Cameras captured the people as they jostled to get to the front of the crowd.

Someone from the crowd yelled "henrymaddox.com," and others responded by shouting "freedom." The chant multiplied to the point where the energy of the once confused crowd was channeled into a cause.

Those in the crowd elevated their cell phones to take pictures and video. Within minutes, these images were uploaded to YouTube, blogs, and other social media outlets.

The counter of registered members began to climb. The buzz about henrymaddox.com had begun.

After an hour of answering questions from the media, Henry and Laroy retired to Henry's on-campus office. The office resembled every other office on the fourth floor of the business building.

"Okay, here it is," said Henry. "Let's see if my key still works."

Henry turned the key and the door opened.

"Well, it's just as I remember it. Now I recall why I don't spend much time on campus."

The cinderblock office walls had faded from the original white to a lusterless cream. Only a couple of books were on the office shelves. No pictures were on the desk and nothing hung on the walls. The office had one window overlooking a campus street.

"I apologize for the Spartan accommodations, Laroy."

"I've seen worse." Laroy sat down in a wooden chair that wobbled when he shifted from side to side. Henry positioned himself behind an oak desk, put his feet up, and looked at Laroy.

"The truth is Laroy, I don't remember the last time I came into this office. I have a key I gave to my graduate assistants so they could use it. I don't even know if they come in here, though. It's kind of depressing, isn't it? I suppose coming back here brings me back to my roots. To think, I would still be here if it were not for my consulting practice."

"Henry, I want to thank you for organizing the event today. I think it really was an astounding success. How did you ever get so many media types interested in the event?"

"I have a public relations firm I used to get the word out. The media are essentially lemmings. If they hear one station is going to pick up the story, all of the others follow suit. So all we really needed was one reputable station to cover it and the others followed. We lucked out a bit in that it was a slow news day. We should get some pretty good coverage."

"Well, slow news day or not, we sure whipped that crowd up into a frenzy."

"That crowd was a nice touch wasn't it?"

"What do you mean 'nice touch?'"

"Oh, I guess I should tell you. I hired a company who specializes in Astroturfing to assemble those people and create all of that ruckus outside the auditorium."

"Astroturfing?"

"I'm sorry. I sometimes lose track of the line between jargon and real-people language. You know what a grassroots movement is right?"

"Sure. Support for a cause that's spontaneous and natural."

"And you know what Astroturf is right?"

"It's fake grass."

"Okay, then you understand. Astroturfing is fake grassroots support. We paid those people to chant – not all of them, but enough of them to provide the perception that the crowd was really energized by your cause."

"How many people did we pay?"

"Probably twenty or thirty, but it's amazing how those few people can really get a crowd going."

"Well there were definitely more than thirty people there. There must have been at least five thousand, don't you think? So the Astroturfers can't explain all of the excitement, right?"

"Actually, the Astroturfers combined with our crowd attraction strategies would explain most of it."

"Crowd attraction strategies?"

"Techniques to leverage the psychology of why people assemble in groups."

"Okay . . ."

"Look, when you go to a movie theater and see people waiting in a line that is wrapped around the building, what's the first thing you do?"

"I ask someone in line what movie they're waiting for."

"Exactly. And chances are you start making plans to see that movie next time you come to the theater. This strategy has been used for store openings as well. You pay twenty people to camp overnight for a store opening or product launch, and pretty soon, you have a couple of hundred people camping along with them. The news outlets love to pickup these types of stories, so these strategies tend to generate some pretty good buzz."

"So you're telling me the twenty or thirty Astroturfers attracted a crowd that ultimately numbered in the thousands?"

"The Astroturfers were part of it. I also specified where I wanted all of the television trucks to park. The television trucks were what turned people's heads. Then the fact that the Astroturfers were energized and waiting around caused people to assemble."

"Henry, I don't know what to say. I was feeling good about our launch but now it seems it was all . . . smoke and mirrors."

"No, it was just marketing. You hired me to fight fire with fire. You told me yourself that your techniques had become outdated. You wondered how you could connect. I'm connecting. Don't get a weak stomach on me, now."

Henry pulled his laptop out of his shoulder bag and launched a browser.

"Laroy look at the noise we've generated for henrymaddox.com. Our views on YouTube, Tumblr, and Reddit are amongst the highest for the day, and our trajectory is impressive. We'll be amongst the most popular stories of the week."

"Did you pay people to vote for us on those sites?"

"We did hire a firm that specializes in maximizing our visibility, but that's not the point Laroy. The takeaway is that our product launch was successful, and not because your message resonated. It was successful because people perceived that it resonated. Do you understand the distinction?"

"No, not really."

"Good. That's the right answer because perception is reality. Laroy, I want you to go home and feel good about what we accomplished today. Your efforts may not ultimately succeed, but it won't be because of me and it certainly won't be because of today. You'll receive massive hits to the website. It's now up to you to convert them."

There is no political solution
To our troubled evolution

- The Police
"Spirits in the Material World" (1981)

CHAPTER 15

The Next Day

An alert on Pressley's smart phone interrupted her breakfast.

"What is it?" her mom asked.

"Hold on one second." Pressley opened her bag and pulled out her laptop. "I just got the first tweet from @henry_maddox."

"Your Professor is tweeting now?"

"It's not exactly coming from Professor Maddox. It's coming from henrymaddox.com."

"It sounds like a distinction without a difference Pressley."

"It gets a little confusing, Mom. A client of Professor Maddox has launched a campaign that uses the free market to improve communities. The first target of the campaign was going to be released today. I wanted to get on the website to see what they had to say."

"And?"

Pressley opened up a browser on her laptop and accessed henrymaddox.com. The home page showed the words "Too Big to Fail" with a circle surrounding the words and a line drawn through it. Pressley read the release aloud to her mother.

> Over the past several years, enormous 'too big to fail' banks have become even larger. Trillions of taxpayer dollars have been infused into these banks in order to keep them afloat. The government justified these bailouts by saying that, without these extreme measures, we would suffer a global financial meltdown. The financial system was so reliant on these banks that the government decided to spare the banks from the consequences of their licentious business practices at your and my expense.

> Today, the top five banks control more than fifty percent of the banking system. While big banks have grown, small banks have suffered. New, massive bank regulations that purport to prevent this type of systemic failure in the future have increased regulatory burdens on the small banks to the point that they can no longer compete.

> Here at henrymaddox.com, we have a bold solution. We are going to do the government and the taxpayers a favor. We want to reduce the size of these big banks so they are no longer 'too

big to fail.' At the same time, we want to encourage the support of the smaller community banks and credit unions that do most of the small business lending in this country. We want to see the exorbitant salaries of the big banking executives replaced by more jobs in the local community banks. We look to capitalism for the solution.

DO YOUR PART: If you have an account at one of the top five banks, we want you to withdraw your money and close out your accounts immediately. You then can open an account at a smaller bank of your choosing. Collectively, henrymaddox.com followers can strengthen communities, lower tax payer obligations, encourage competition, and restore respectability to our financial system.

"Destruction is not profit."
– Frederic Bastiat (1850)

The text was followed by a video. Pressley clicked on the link. Laroy Elden was seated in a chair in what looked to be a home office.

"Hello, this is Laroy Elden. As many of you know, yesterday we launched our new website henrymaddox.com to organize and motivate people who are interested in strengthening our communities. Too many families have either lost their homes or seen their property values plummet as a consequence of the irresponsible lending practices of the Federal Government and major banks.

Governments and large financial institutions got us into this mess. So why are we looking to them to get us out of it?

"We're calling on all individuals to withdraw your money from the big five banks and instead begin a business relationship with a local bank or credit union. Only by doing this will we show both our government and the banking industry that they're in business to serve us – not manipulate us.

"As this is our first cause, we're looking to you to make this a success. As Professor Henry Maddox would say, 'we want to move the needle.' Only then will our collective voice have influence. Thank you."

"Mom, call Dad," Pressley said. "We need to close our accounts and reopen them at a local credit union."

"Pressley we're not going to let your Professor dictate where we do our banking."

"This isn't Professor Maddox, it's Laroy Elden. He started Save Our Families to promote procommunity values. He's a decent person and I believe in what he's doing."

Pressley's mom remained silent.

"Mom, this is a big deal to me. Please do this. We can make a difference."

"Okay, I'll call your father."

"And then call and email everyone you know."

"Pressley, I'm not going to stake my reputation on this."

"But you're okay with forwarding chain letter spam? Wouldn't you say this is more legitimate?"

"You never know when those chain emails might pay-off Pressley. I just figure it's better to be safe than sorry."

"Okay, you have no credibility when it comes to establishing rules about forwarding email. I'll send you an email with the link to henrymaddox.com and you'll forward it to your entire address book. Okay?"

"Oh, all right."

"Promise?"

"Promise."

"Pinky swear?"

"Pressley . . ."

"Okay, never mind."

"You know, I haven't seen you this excited about anything for a while."

"For too long I've looked to older people to leave me a better world. They've done nothing but leave my generation with a mountain of debt and a messed up government. Starting today, I'm taking control. This isn't about politics. This is about morality and *my* future."

———

Henry spent the morning on the phone with clients. As a courtesy, he called to notify them of the henrymaddox.com campaign and let them know it was an experiment of sorts and they should in no way feel threatened. Most of the clients appreciated the call. They weren't happy about the campaign, but they were willing to believe that, as long as he was in charge, they had nothing to fear.

Henry went to his office in the early afternoon. As soon as he came through the door, Cheryl erupted with enthusiasm. "Henry, you have got to see the analytics that henrymaddox.com is pulling in. I've been checking them all morning. The number of registrants cracked six figures at about eleven thirty."

"Seriously? Fantastic."

"We're all over the internet. All the major news websites and blogs have picked us up as one of their leads."

"This isn't just Astroturf, Cheryl. We have a legitimate grassroots campaign on our hands. Points to Laroy for picking a winner as his first cause. This should really grow his base."

"I guess the main measure of success will be to see if the large banks take notice of any significant defection."

"That would be Laroy's measure of success. Ours is the size of the registration list. Remember, we're gathering as much information about them as possible. It's all in the data."

"Should we then be asking for more user information? We're currently asking for just names, email addresses, and phone numbers."

"Typically, I'd say no. It would be too early. We would need to create more trust with our users before asking for anything that would be considered personal. But since this is a campaign and our users are united against a common cause, I think we already enjoy a high level of trust. We can use that."

"So what do you want to do?"

"First, post on the website how pleased we are with the overwhelming reception of our website – which is absolutely true. Tell them they're making a difference – which is probably true. Make something up about the major banks contacting us and asking us to take down our site. This will energize the activism. Next, tell our registrants that for security reasons we're now asking our users to login to the system with a password. This will make them feel safe and exclusive. Then, ask each user to expand their personal profile. We'll begin to develop these true believers into an online community. They'll bond with each other as they share personal experiences and details in discussion forums. Ask them to invite their friends to the groups to support the cause.

"Once we have these people login to our website, we can track their behaviors. We'll know which pages they click on and how long they stay. We can expand the website to have sponsor pages. We can track which types of products and services attract which types of users. We can start to identify the types of correlations that exist within the data of these activists. This is where the data gets valuable."

"I'll get right on it," Cheryl said. "Our developers should be able to get the framework up by tomorrow."

"You see how easy it can be to run a business, Cheryl?"

"Ha. This business *has* been very good to us both."

"It sure beats punching a clock somewhere doesn't it? And to think, we've only just begun."

We live, in fact,
in a world starved for
solitude, silence, and privacy,
and therefore starved for
meditation and true friendship.

- C.S. Lewis
"The Weight of Glory"

CHAPTER 16

The knock at the door came at eleven o'clock in the morning. Margaret Elden wiped her hands against an already stained apron before she reached for the knob. On the other side of the door was a pleasant-looking man in a black turtleneck, tweed jacket, and khakis. It was almost a caricature of a professorial outfit, but was saved from self-parody by the quality of the materials – she was pretty sure the turtleneck was a silk blend – and the ease with which he wore them.

"Hello," he said, "I'm here to see Laroy Elden. My name is Henry Maddox."

"Of course Henry, my name is Margaret. I'm Laroy's wife. I'd shake your hand but my hands are a little messy right now. Please come in and have a seat."

Margaret led Henry to the kitchen table. "Can I get you something to eat or drink?"

"No, thank you. I just ate."

"Very well. Laroy will be down in just a moment. He had some phone calls he was attending to that I think put him behind a bit."

"I don't mind waiting. It smells delicious in here."

Margaret resumed chopping carrots on a cutting board. "I'm in the middle of making a stew. With our kids now out of the house, I find myself making easy meals that I can stretch over several days."

"I guess that makes for a simpler life."

"Simpler yes but I sure miss my children. My home went from complete chaos to absolute silence in what seemed like a week. It's a shame there isn't a happy medium."

"I guess I can't comment much on that dynamic."

"Yes, Laroy told me that you're single, no children. You don't believe much in family?"

"My life works for me."

Margaret dropped her carrots into the pot, added a couple of bay leaves, and crushed in a couple of cloves of garlic. It was several minutes before she turned back to Maddox.

"You don't believe Laroy's cause, do you Henry?"

Henry paused a moment, clearly crafting his response.

"I don't see it as my job to believe in his cause. My job is to generate traffic to the website. If Laroy's efforts are successful, I'll be happy for him."

"So you're essentially amoral?"

"I wouldn't say that. I don't think there's anything wrong in what I do. Though I'd guess I see morality as less clearly defined than you do."

Margaret washed her hands and then sat down across the kitchen table from Henry. "Do you enjoy literature Henry?"

"When I read it. Most of what I read is in my field."

"After my daughter passed," Margaret said, "I started taking classes at the University. I particularly enjoy studying the classics. Reading the great authors provides an extraordinary view into the past. Great authors place us in another time, with different customs, comforts, and concerns. Have you ever read The Brothers Karamazov?"

"Dostoevsky? No I don't believe that I have. Why?"

"It's just that you remind me of one of his characters. Would you excuse me for a minute?"

Margaret went into the den and found her worn Penguin Classics copy of the book.

"You must excuse me Henry. I know you didn't come here to hear a book report, but I hope that this may be of some interest to you."

A forced smile parted Maddox's lips. "You have a captive audience Margaret. I guess I might as well learn something."

"First, you need to understand, Fyodor Dostoevsky was born as the second of seven children to a family in Moscow, Russia. His father was a doctor who worked at the Mariinksy Hospital for the Poor in Moscow. The hospital was located near a cemetery for criminals, a lunatic asylum, and an orphanage for abandoned infants – not exactly the best part of town. This area made a lasting impression on young Fyodor as he grew up. He spent time with the patients growing up and developed a compassion for the mentally and materially less fortunate. At sixteen, his mother died of tuberculosis. He was then sent to a military institute in St. Petersburg. Fyodor's father died two years later, when he was only eighteen.

"At the military institute, Fyodor developed a love for literature. He studied Shakespeare, Pascal, Victor Hugo, and E.T.A. Hoffman. He began to write, developed a following, and became somewhat of a celebrity at only twenty-four. His literary circles aligned him with a liberal intellectual group that promoted the thoughts of a French utopian socialist named Charles Fourier, which led to Fyodor opposing the tsarist autocracy and the Russian serfdom. He advocated atheistic communism because he thought the church and the Tsar conspired to keep the lower classes in poverty. In 1848, revolutions across fifty countries – extending from Europe to parts of Latin America – caused a brief, Europe-wide collapse of traditional authority. Nicholas I didn't want a similar fate to occur in Russia. As a precautionary, preventative measure Tsar Nicholas sentenced Fyodor along with some of his liberal intellectual comrades to death.

"So at 28-years-old, Fyodor had gone from fame to standing outside in the freezing weather, waiting to be executed by a firing squad. At the last moment, Tsar Nicholas stopped the execution and instead sentenced him to four years of exile and hard labor at a prison camp in Siberia.

"Allow me to read from a letter Fyodor sent to his brother about his time in Siberia."

Margaret opened to the book's preface.

"'In summer, intolerable closeness; in winter, unendurable cold. All the floors were rotten. Filth on the floors an inch thick; one could slip and fall... We were packed like herrings in a barrel . . . There was no room to turn around. From dusk to dawn it was impossible not to behave like pigs . . . Fleas, lice, and black beetles by the bushel . . .'"

"Wow," Henry said with apparent sincerity.

"He was released from prison when he was 32 years old. While in prison, Fyodor had time to think and one book – The Bible. He converted to Christianity and turned against the Nihilist and Socialist movements he once embraced. In social circles, he surrounded himself with well known conservatives. The man's writing took on a new depth as he focused on existential themes such as spiritual torment, religious awakening, and the psychological confusion caused by the mixing of traditional and modern cultures. Although his insights are over 130 years old, they are as applicable to our current day as if they were written yesterday."

Margaret opened the novel to a marked page and scanned the text before settling on a passage.

"'He was not a young man and he was certainly intelligent. He was just as sincere as you are, although he spoke in an amused tone, with a sort of bitter humor. 'I love mankind,' he said, 'but I find to my amazement that the more I love mankind as a whole, the less I love individual people. In my thoughts,' the doctor told me, 'I often visualize ecstatically the sacrifices I could make for mankind and, indeed, I might even accept martyrdom for my fellow men if circumstances suddenly demanded it of me. In actual fact, however, I cannot bear to spend two days in the same room with another person. And this I know from personal experience. Whenever someone is too close to me, I feel my personal dignity and freedom are being infringed upon. Within twenty-four hours I can come to hate the best of men, perhaps because he eats too slowly or because he has a cold and keeps blowing his nose. I become a man's enemy,' he said, 'as soon as he touches me. But to make up for it, the more I hate individual people, the more ardent is my general love for mankind.'

She closed the book. "I love that insight because it speaks to the true nature of love – especially as it exists within a family. It's specific, unrelenting, and unconditional. This type of love transforms the giver and the receiver. Parents, children, and siblings learn patience, kindness, tolerance, and selflessness as they find ways to resolve conflict within their homes. This type of love is not sexy and it certainly isn't easy. If everyone concentrated on their own sphere of influence rather than being carried away in some more celebrated, esoteric cause, the world would be a much kinder place."

"No doubt," Henry said with a polite smile that looked well-practiced.

"I've always tried to ask myself the question, 'what would the world be like if everyone was like me . . . if every family was like mine?' You see Henry, *that* is true accountability. One's influence grows organically. I need to actively love the people I encounter on a daily basis . . . not save up my love for one well attended, heroic deed, which may never come.

"It wasn't until recently that I understood an added depth to Dostoevsky's insight. In 1765, the author of an anonymous article in a French Enlightenment periodical said the following:

"The *general love of humanity* . . . a virtue hitherto quite nameless among us, and which we will venture to call '*humanism*', for the time has come to create a word for such a beautiful and necessary thing.'

"You see, Dostoevsky was taking a jab at 'humanism' when he postulated that the 'general love for mankind' was a copout. 'Humanism' contended that human virtue could be created by reason alone, and that any thought of transcendent moral absolutes was nonsense. Notably, Karl Marx embraced the philosophy of 'humanism' as he criticized the close involvement of the church in the repressive German government. Marx's 'Das Kapital' was published in 1867, and the first foreign publication of the work appeared in Russia in 1872. The first print run of 'Das Kapital' sold out in Russia within one year. 'The Brothers Karamazov' was published in 1880. Unfortunately, Dostoevsky died only four months after 'The Brothers Karamazov' was published. As a former atheistic socialist himself, Dostoevsky had thought through the consequences of Marx's philosophies – as well as humanism in general – and sounded a warning to his beloved Russia in his last great work.

"We now know the soul crushing impact that atheistic, humanistic, and socialistic philosophies had on the people of Russia. Henry, as we neglect moral absolutes, history has taught us that the consequences are swift and brutal."

Henry ran his fingers through his dark, cropped hair. "With all due respect Margaret, I don't aspire to die for some great and noble cause. I don't pretend to even love mankind in general. I recognize and accept my own limits."

"I understand that. My point is that each of us is accountable for our actions. These insights have influenced me personally. They have made me more aware of my behavior each day. Our daily conduct changes the people we encounter as well as us."

"Sorry I kept you waiting, Henry." Laroy strode into the kitchen. "I see you've met Margaret."

"Yes. We were just chatting about literature."

"She's certainly good at that," Laroy said. "I better save you before she starts in on Tolstoy and logical positivism. Let's come into the living room to discuss the campaign."

Henry stood up and began to follow Laroy, then stopped and turned. "Margaret?"

"Yes, Henry?"

"You began your discussion about Dostoevsky by telling me that I reminded you of one of his characters, but the passage you shared didn't seem to apply to me specifically."

"Oh, yes. I was thinking of the father of the Karamazov sons." Margaret opened the book and thumbed to a highlighted passage. "Dostoevsky said that he was a man that belonged, quote, '. . . to a peculiar though widespread human type, the sort of man who is not only wretched and depraved but also muddle-headed – muddle-headed in a way that allows him to pull off all sorts of shady little financial deals and not much else.'" She closed the book. "Henry, life is about more than money. Ultimately the people you affect will be your legacy."

Henry nodded. He then left the kitchen to catch up with Laroy.

Henry entered Laroy's small but comfortable living room and sat down. From early wedding pictures of Laroy and Margaret to recent family pictures including grandchildren, a photographic history of the Elden family covered the walls.

Laroy noticed him looking at them. "You know, I can't seem to remember where I put my car keys anymore, but I certainly remember all of the details of each one of these photographs." Laroy pointed to a framed family portrait. "You see that one right there?"

"The one with all of you in pastel colors and white pants?"

"It was the eighties. I put up the biggest fight with the photographer over that one. She wanted everyone in bare feet and I refused. You see how I'm the only one with shoes on? My children still tease me about that to this day. And look at this one over here. You see how my oldest son has orange hair? Well his hair is naturally brown but he put lemon juice on it over the summer to see if he could bleach it blonde. You can see the results. As a family, we told him all summer how great he looked. We didn't tell him the truth until he asked if he should do it again the next summer."

Laroy gleamed with pride.

"And this one here?" Maddox asked.

"That is of my late daughter Jenny." Laroy lingered at the photo. "Such a special girl . . ."

He couldn't help but think of what Margaret had just said. But he kept telling himself that he was doing this for a good cause – the discovery of an untapped market. "You've created quite a legacy for yourself."

"Don't get me started Henry. I've a hard time being modest when it comes to my family. Let's talk about the campaign."

Henry and Laroy sat down on either side of a coffee table.

"I brought over some of the key analytics from the website Laroy. The specific categories and numbers may not mean much to you. They're only meaningful when you put them in context."

Laroy scanned the page. "I see what you mean. What's the 'bounce rate?'"

"To put all of this in simple terms Laroy, our response on the website is nothing short of amazing. We now have over five hundred thousand people registered. All of these people follow us on Twitter. We're experiencing over one hundred thousand hits a day, with about half of those coming from new visitors. The people who come to our site are evenly dispersed throughout the country, and most of those who visit us stay for a long time. In short, you've got the nation's attention.

"This leads me to my next subject. Our data shows that your visitors are hungry for more content. If we had more to show them, people would stay longer. So I've decided to expand the site to include more features. To make the site safer as well as enrich the user experience, we have now included the ability to log in to our site. We have message boards where visitors can share experiences and collaborate. We've added surveys that allow our users to provide us with more of their personal information. This will allow us to increase our following to reach more people like them. Because of the demand, we've included a sponsor page that links to other partner sites – at the moment, a lot of smaller, community focused banks. People can enter a zip code and find the small bank nearest to them."

"This all sounds wonderful Henry, but do we know if our cause is making any impact?"

"*That* is hard to know. The big banks don't exactly disclose their customer attrition rate. Many smaller banks have advertised that they're opening new accounts since our campaign launched, but we don't have any way to verify it."

"So what's next?"

"We need to continue this momentum. It's been three weeks since we first launched the site. We need another cause, and I want you to think big."

"I'll get something to you by the end of the week."

Laroy walked Henry to the door. "You know, Henry, I appreciate what you're doing."

"I'm enjoying it. Let's see if you can make a difference."

*Sunlight is said
to be the best of disinfectants;
electric light
the most efficient policeman.*

- Louis Brandeis (1913)

CHAPTER 17

Pressley was on the train, on her way to school when her phone buzzed. She still had ten minutes left before she arrived at the Berkeley BART station, not enough time to dig out the e-reader and power it up, so a message was a welcome diversion. It was a Tweet from henrymaddox.com.

> Which family friendly brand derives massive profit from pornography? Visit henrymaddox.com to find out. #destructionisnotprofit

Pressley clicked on the henrymaddox.com hyperlink on her smart phone. A browser opened and she waited for the website to load. An image of Bell Cable Systems appeared on the screen covered by the word "pornographers" in a spray painted graffiti font. Pressley read the copy below the image.

Did you know that the world's largest satellite and cable companies are also among the biggest beneficiaries of pornography profits? Not that this fact shows up on their financial reports. Why? Because they bury these profits underneath a sophisticated conglomerate structure and ultimately disclose them only as 'Partner Revenues.'

This issue is about more than pornography, it's about transparency and accountability. A corporation should not be able to enjoy the benefits of a community-friendly brand while profiting off of subsidiaries that destroy the family. In an age where corporations know more and more about their consumers; consumers know less and less about corporations. Here at henrymaddox.com, we think it's time for this to change.

DO YOUR PART: Over the next couple of weeks, we will profile companies that secretly profit off of unsavory and destructive practices. We'll name names and encourage boycotts. We will also highlight businesses that have consciously avoided destructive revenue streams despite their competitors taking advantage of these sources of income.

"Destruction is not profit."
- Frederic Bastiat (1850)"

Pressley arrived at the Berkeley station, strapped on her backpack, and headed for campus. She was excited about the direction the henrymaddox.com campaigns were taking but still would have liked to be more involved. She had a couple of hours before her first class. Pressley knew Professor Maddox's consulting office wasn't far from the BART station. It was time to do something bold.

Pressley weaved through pedestrian traffic as she navigated Center Street. Even after three years at Berkeley, she still wasn't immune to the neighborhood's contrasts. Wealthy yuppies brunched at chic restaurants while homeless people slept on park benches. Students bustled around internet cafes while aging hippies played the role of troubadours to an indifferent audience. Berkeley seemed an evolving experiment in how diverse people could coexist. Or, as Professor Maddox would probably see it, an exercise in fragmentation.

Pressley had never been to Professor Maddox's consulting office but she knew roughly where it was. Students often spoke about the office's location with what seemed like a fabled reverence. She got to Berkeley's art district and turned left by a Brazilian capoeira club. There, in the shadows of a contemporary apartment building was a small residential structure. Pressley inspected the smoked glass on the front door of the old, restored home but couldn't locate any signage. She twisted the doorknob and opened the door.

"Can I help you?" A woman asked as she poked her head around the door.

"I apologize for not having an appointment" Pressley said, "but I'm one of Professor Maddox's students. I was hoping I could have a word with him."

"I'm sorry, but Professor Maddox only sees students on campus and only during his published office hours."

"My visit actually has nothing to do with his class. It has to do with the 'Destruction Is Not Profit' campaign."

"And your name is?"

"Pressley Hamil."

"Alright Ms. Hamil, let me see if he'll see you."

Within minutes Maddox walked into the reception area. As he approached, doubts overtook her, but it was too late to back out now.

"Hello Ms. Hamil, how can I help you?"

"Professor Maddox sir, I apologize for visiting you off campus, but I felt I needed to speak with you."

Maddox waited while Pressley gathered her thoughts.

"I don't know if you remember me from class or not. I know you have a lot of students. Your class made me think about a lot of different things. Quite frankly, it upset me a great deal . . . that is until recently. I want to compliment you on your participation with Laroy Elden on the henrymaddox.com campaign. I registered online and I consider myself an active follower of the cause."

"Well thank you for coming by and letting us know that Ms. Hamil. Is that all?"

"No, no it isn't. I came here this morning to ask if I can help with the campaigns."

As she said this, all of Pressley's rehearsed supporting arguments escaped her. She fell back into an awkward silence.

"We currently aren't hiring, but if you leave your name with Cheryl we will keep you in mind as opportunities arise."

No. She couldn't go without a fight. This cause meant too much. She could make a difference.

"I'll work for free, Professor Maddox. I'll work as much or as little as you want. I just want to help and learn. You can ask me to leave at any time and I will, with no questions. You certainly must have some filing to do around here or something. I'll even clean the office if you want me to."

"Ms. Hamil, I've got to admire your audacity, but I'm not sure we have anything for you to do. We maintain a high level of confidentiality with our clients. This would prohibit you from assisting with any meaningful work we might have."

"What if she could work exclusively on Laroy's campaign?" Cheryl asked. "I'm sure that he won't mind. He seems like the type who would want to mentor a young person like Ms. Hamil. Besides, we're expanding the site, and I could use someone who could help to coordinate with all our development consultants. As a henrymaddox.com follower herself, Ms. Hamil could provide some helpful input."

"Okay fine, you sold me," Maddox said. "Get Laroy's approval and you can use Ms. Hamil on the campaigns. I'll need some references though. Ms Hamil, why don't you leave your contact information with Cheryl, and she'll get back to you."

"Thank you Professor. I'm a good worker. You won't be disappointed."

A week later, Henry and Cheryl met to discuss the henrymaddox.com website. The number of website visitors was growing at an impressive pace. Laroy's recent campaign to hold conglomerates accountable for all of their subsidiaries proved to be a perfect follow-up to his first "too big to fail" campaign. The henrymaddox.com discussion forums were keeping users engaged and on the site. The average time on site per user had increased to an enviable thirteen minutes. The audience demographics of the site tended to skew to the middle aged, with the majority of the visitors from 35 to 54 years-old. Visitors overwhelmingly had some level of college education. Users also tended to be more female than male.

Maddox leveraged the recent analytics findings to try to monetize the website, soliciting ads from companies that fit the demographics. Although the site traffic was strong and advertisements were well positioned for the targeted demographics, pay per click conversions were unimpressive. In more simple terms, henrymaddox.com users were not interested in buying products. They were only interested in promoting a cause.

"This has always been the problem with these more stable demographics," Henry said. "They consume information but they don't buy products." Why would any company want to produce any content for these people? It was so much easier to sell to the younger and less educated.

"So what do you suggest?" Cheryl asked.

"Well, it's Laroy controlling the message, so we can't alter the content of the site to attract different users. When you review the data analytics, what segments stand out?"

"Over eighty-five percent of the users have children."

"Of those that have children, how many of these fall within the 35 to 44 year-old age group?"

"Thirty-five percent."

"Okay, if we're going to fragment the market, we want to start here." Typically the younger the demographic, the more easily fragmented. This age group will be more influenced by media messaging. "How many in this group are mothers."

"Seventy percent."

"And what is their annual household income?"

"Seventy-five thousand a year."

"Above the national average – good – this shows consumption potential. With young families, however, we're fighting with other priorities for those dollars – rainy day savings, college savings, after school activities and such. We need a compelling message that attracts young mothers."

"The comments from young mothers' on the message boards talk a lot about how much time they put into their families – to the point where they feel isolated and disconnected."

This was looking promising. But these young mothers were mostly educated, so he needed to be subtle. He needed to exalt motherhood while encouraging comparison. "Let's amplify the social media component of the website. Allow for more expansive content – photos and videos. Each user should have her own home page. Mothers need to correspond with other mothers on the site. They can share the most mundane of child raising experiences while others offer support and encouragement." And these young mothers would naturally want to compare their family experiences with others.

"But why would a mother want to share with thousands of people who she doesn't know?"

"At first they won't. But as others do it, they'll catch on."

"So the trick is to get a number of mothers to get the ball rolling."

"Exactly. We'll seed the posts."

"What do you mean seed the posts?"

"The first post will be from the Peterson family who live in San Diego, California. They have five kids, all equally spaced. Their oldest is a sixteen year-old girl, followed by a fourteen year-old boy, a twelve year-old boy, and twin ten year-old girls. All of the children are beautiful, smart, and happy – you should see the photos. And the parents, Russ and Diana, look like they just stepped out of a catalog. There's no way you would ever think Diana had five kids. But she *did* and her secret to staying in shape is Pilates and eating right."

"What are you talking about? We haven't collected this type of information on our users yet. How would you know this about the Petersons?"

"Easy. I'm making it up. The Peterson family is a fictional ideal. Just to jumpstart the process." And young mothers would compare their family to this perfect family and feel inferior. The next step would be to test different product links aimed at bridging these young mothers' insecurities. Other mothers will want to compete with the attention of the Peterson family and use the blog to show how spectacular their family is too. They'll share valuable personal information about their families without us even having to ask. These legitimate blog entries would self-perpetuate the campaign. He could just sit back and watch where the mothers take the blogs.

Henry shook himself out of his stream of consciousness. "We'll allow users to contribute comments to each blog entry. We'll seed the first comments as well to create the tone of the discussion for the remaining users. 'There's no way you had five kids including twins Diana! You look so great!' You get the picture."

"I'm not entirely certain that I understand your marketing angle. Where's the fragmentation?"

He wasn't sure yet, but there had to be a disruptive force – a wedge that fragments.

"We'll have to wait for the data," Henry said. Yes, the answers were all in the data.

Consumed with that
which it was nourished by.

- Shakespeare, "Sonnet 73"

CHAPTER 18

Two weeks had passed since Henry devised the strategy to fragment young mothers. A faux family had been created with the express intent of making real life mothers feel inadequate. The fake mother, Diana Peterson, was beautiful, fit, and intelligent, with inexhaustible energy.

The first of Diana's blog entries spoke of how she stayed up until midnight baking her twelve year-old son a birthday cake. Pictures showed a professionally decorated, football themed, cake. The San Diego Chargers lightning bolt was emblazoned on the cake with an assortment of the Charger's star players surrounding the decorative emblem. Each of the players were edible and made to scale.

Detailed instructions on how Diana made the cake were incorporated into the blog. As Diana mentioned on the blog, ". . . the cake took me twelve hours, but it was my first time. If you follow my directions, you should be able to finish the cake in fewer than ten."

An amateurish looking video showed how her twelve year-old son, Braxton, was overjoyed when he saw the cake.

"You're the awesomest mom ever!" The camera caught the father, Russ, as he gave Diana a kiss and said, "I'm so lucky to be married to you." The video then ended.

Comments on the bottom of the blog regaled Diana with praise.

"I don't know how you do it Diana." – MissyO

"Wow, you should do this type of thing professionally!" – Joygirl24

"I had the same experience when I baked a cake for my son. Wasn't it fun?" – Natalie

"My football figures didn't turn out as good as yours. How were you able to make the jerseys look so good?" – LisaR

"This blog is such a good idea. I just started one for myself. Click here to see my first entry." – BrittanyAZ

All of them had been written by Henry.

Brittany (another fictional mother) then had a blog that featured a stunning family photo with her, her husband, and six children – all under twelve. Her first entry spoke of how she was training for a triathlon. Because her life was so busy, she had to get up at four o'clock every morning to swim at the local fitness club. She was encouraged, however, because she just ran five miles in under seven minute mile splits. She had a photo of her chiseled body running as the sun was coming up over Camelback Mountain in Scottsdale, Arizona.

Henry crafted the initial comments in Brittany's blog as well. As Henry had hoped, comments began to flood in from real life mothers. Henry cross referenced each comment to the user's profile and confirmed they were reaching their targeted 35 to 44 year-old target demographic.

Within a couple of days, legitimate blogs from mothers began to surface. Each blog posting added another criterion to what began to form into an image of the perfect young mother. The super mom was skilled at child-raising, an ideal homemaker, physically fit, fashionable, intellectually stimulating, informed on the latest child-raising techniques, the apples of their husband's eye, and adored by her children. Of course, the real life blogs were as close to fiction as the faux blogs. No mother spoke of spending the day cleaning up after a child with the flu and dreaming of an adult conversation. No mother spoke of fears of losing the part-time job at the bookstore or worries about making the mortgage. Legitimate conversation happened between real friends, not virtual voyeurs. Henry monitored the data closely as participation increased and the ideal mother continued to evolve. The ideal remained a moving target that could never be reached.

Henry had set the hook and was ready to reel them in. He identified several areas of product promotion and went to work courting advertisers. The blogs soon displayed pay-per-click ads for energy and weight loss supplements, fitness apparel, beauty products, parenting resources, self-help books, children's videos, vacation destinations, and restaurants.

The ad revenue on henrymaddox.com began to grow. Henry had accomplished his first goal; he had monetized the website. He had identified a demographic and persuaded it to start spending money. More encouraging to Henry, however, was that he began to see the potential for fragmentation.

Enthusiastic, Henry called Cheryl into his office.

"Have you noticed the commonality between the products that are selling on the blogs?"

"Well, they're all aimed at bridging the gap between the ideal mother and the real life mother." She sat down next to him to have a closer look at his monitor. "Typical marketing stuff, right?"

"Sure," Henry said, "but if you look closer at the data, many of the purchases are coming from users that have maxed out their income. These mothers are so compelled by our messaging that they're willing to spend their last dollar to achieve the ideal."

"So what are you thinking?"

"Rather than continue to sell product, which yields only a nominal return, this is our chance to fragment the market. Don't forget that this whole exercise with Laroy isn't about selling a couple of widgets on a website. The experiment is to see if we can take community minded citizens – people with self respect – and divide them into more profitable markets. We want to *create* needs that these users didn't know they had. If we can do this, we will have cornered a tremendous, untapped market."

Henry stood up. He grabbed a piece of paper, crumpled it up and shot it into a waste basket ten feet away. "Score."

"And you think that exploiting maxed out mothers is your key to unlocking this potential?"

"The formula's worked before, Cheryl. Create an ideal, see how your target responds by monitoring the data, wait for your opportunity, and then act. This is our chance."

"Henry, listen . . . instead of fragmenting a new market, can't we just show Laroy how to create a profitable website that supports a good cause? He can use our research to reach out to young mothers and support them, not exploit them."

"But we need to follow the market. I'm only being rational."

"So what would this mean?"

"Look, so far we've identified market needs but we haven't created any new markets. The new markets will be created as we target those young mothers who can't afford to buy what they perceive they need. The trap, as it were, will be the next step."

"Trap?"

"I've partnered with a credit card company that exchanges easy qualification for high interest rates. These cash strapped mothers will finance their way to perfect motherhood."

"I still don't see it. The desperate mother? Is that your new market?"

"I don't love this angle either, but remember this is just an experiment. And we've won. Winter or Hoffman could never do what we've just done. Follow me for a second. As the accumulated debt grows and becomes a burden to the household, relationship difficulties ensue – the husband blames the wife for their financial problems. The financial stress ultimately separates the family. Two households are created out of one."

"Both of which are financially destitute. Where are the new markets when neither home has any money to spend?"

"The mother, out of necessity, begins to work outside of the home. This extra income ultimately increases the aggregate income of the two households above the prior single family home. Household consumption increases in previously untapped markets. Instead of the children getting braces, that money will now be spent on child care. Food consumption changes from home-made meals to fast food. The consequences of the break-up of one nuclear family will be felt exponentially through extended families and communities. Extended families must now provide emotional and financial support to shore up deficiencies. This added strain will compromise extended family relationships while providing an added source of income for new consumption patterns. Can you begin to see all of the new markets that will form?"

"All I see is destruction. Henry, there's nothing good here."

"Cheryl, this is capitalism. I'm not forcing anyone to acquire debt. I'm only providing them with that option."

Cheryl's expression didn't change.

"Listen," he said, "I agree that it wouldn't be prudent for a young mother to acquire debt at such high interest rates, especially to conform to some arbitrary standard."

"That you created."

"All, right, fine. But the decision is still theirs. And for me to deprive these women of the ability to finance their appetites would be to deny them opportunity. Who's to say they wouldn't go off and do this without my introduction to the credit card company? I'm doing them a favor. Intelligent consumers need to know all of their options."

"Henry, are you listening to yourself? You're duping these women, not educating them. You're justifying the unjustifiable."

"So, what are you saying? That they're no longer free? They're not the ones making the decisions that get them in trouble?"

"No, I'm just saying that peer pressure counts. Social norms count. You've used their altruism to suck them into a social group where you surround them with a false ideal, then offer them only bad choices to try to live up to it. Yes, they're still free to opt out of the whole thing, but they won't because they think that everything they see around them – your impossible ideal of motherhood – is just . . . the way things are. Most people don't have the insight to step out of their society, and you know it."

"What has gotten into you all of a sudden? Since when have you decided to take the high road?" He realized he was yelling and turned away to pull himself together. Arguments like this from precocious sophomores were one thing, but Cheryl knew his techniques. She knew him, or he thought she did. But it was beginning to sound like she didn't like what she saw.

He called on years of training to keep his voice steady. "Don't you realize that the millions of dollars you have in the bank are because of my strategies? What do you think we do here? We certainly don't feed the poor and clothe the naked. There's no money in that."

"I know that," she said quietly. "But this is different. When we worked with Melvin Entz, we were just helping him do what he was already doing, but do it better. This will destroy Laroy. It will trash his otherwise impeccable reputation. Good, community minded people will see Laroy as an ignorant fool for trusting you. Do you want that on your conscience?"

"Oh come on Cheryl. He knew who he was hiring–"

"I can't do this, Henry. I can't ruin a good man."

"What are you saying?"

"Henry, I never knew my father, so I've always imagined what a perfect father would be like. Laroy comes closer to that ideal than anyone I've ever met. This is your business. You'll obviously run it as you choose. But if you compromise Laroy's campaign, you'll have to do it without me. I won't help you destroy him."

"Cheryl, are you quitting?"

"I'd rather not, but that's up to you. Allow Laroy to continue his campaign without interference, and keep me, or keep doing what you're doing, without me. It's your call."

It shall even be as when
an hungry man dreameth,
and behold, he eateth;
but he awaketh,
and his soul is empty…

- Isaiah 29:8 (KJV)

CHAPTER **19**

Henry sat on the rooftop deck of his home. It was nearly midnight, and the city was starting to shut down. He watched the shrinking number of cars ascend and descend the undulating streets of San Francisco. He could see the Golden Gate Bridge, the San Francisco Bay, and Alcatraz. Of all the landmarks, he loved the bridge the most; though he identified most with Alcatraz – isolated, alone, abandoned.

When Henry bought the home, he envisioned doing a lot of entertaining. And at first, he did. He enjoyed showing off his new diggs. His clients, partners, and other socialites would gather at his home and compliment him on his charm, intelligence, and business savvy. They would talk about how this house was perfect for him. The view was tremendous they would say . . . very appropriate for a man of such vision. He felt validated.

The novelty of the home soon wore off. Henry's visitors turned out to be mere guests, not friends. Henry grew bored with trying to impress them. When he stopped extending invitations, people stopped visiting.

Henry now rarely spent time anywhere except for the rooftop deck. He enjoyed the atmosphere of the city; the smells, the noise . . . he allowed the bite of the wind to numb his face. All of these sensations reminded him he was alive.

He was alive, of course, clinically speaking. But it wasn't much of a life. He had only one friend, Cheryl. The others just needed him . . . used him. For years he had reasoned that most people were too intimidated by his intellect to grow close. But maybe they just didn't trust him.

Cheryl was right. He was betraying Laroy. Did it take her this long to figure out that he made his living by taking advantage of others?

He filled each day with distractions, gaining admiration from his students and clients. But when he was alone in the merciless night, his conscience was waiting. He'd thought he was handling it well. He was even proud of the way he had avoided the mistakes of his parents.

His father had left the family when he was only ten. Henry was told his parents "had grown apart." He was also told that just because they didn't love each other didn't mean they didn't still love him. Henry believed that for nearly a year. That is when his dad stopped visiting. His father had apparently fallen in love with another woman and then another and another. His mom stopped lying to him and started drinking. They both knew the truth anyway. Henry's father respected no one, not even himself.

A man with self respect would never abandon those he loved. Henry settled on this insight when he was fifteen. It was the first time he began studying people's motives. In a rational world, a person would only trade one thing for another of greater value. Why then did people act irrationally so often? This was the question that wound up shaping his life.

The answers came over time. There were those who lost perspective. Some lacked discipline, some were simply selfish. Far too many were ignorant. But the most imperious, irrational force of all surfaced when his mother began her fight with addiction.

Henry was her mother's only child. She had invested herself entirely to raising him, working sixty hour weeks in a mindless and thankless job. He saw his mother each night and every morning, until the addiction began. Then he hardly saw her at all.

The alcohol began as a therapy – an escape from the otherwise monotonous and dismal grind she called a life. She used to focus on the hope of her life, him. *He* made the sacrifice worth it. As Henry became more independent, however, he needed her less, and she turned to alcohol to soothe her pain.

Her descent accelerated quickly. Within a year she was unemployed, and Henry was living with his grandparents. How could someone who loved him so much become indifferent to him so quickly? Her love for destructive alcohol had replaced her love for anything, everything.

Then seventeen, Henry decided he needed to make it on his own. He graduated from High School and got accepted to Columbia. His dire financial situation and lamentable personal story qualified him for financial grants. Always smart, Henry excelled. But his intelligence wasn't his secret.

His drive was. As others went home for holidays, he studied and worked. In fact, Henry never returned home again, not even for his mother's funeral.

Unlike others his age, he knew what he wanted – an answer to his great question. Why did people act irrationally? He double majored in sociology and psychology and minored in economics. He explored incentives, techniques of persuasion, and habit formation. He kept after the question through graduate school. The significance of his PHD thesis escaped many. He asserted that in present day society, consumption determined identity. As an extension, he claimed that if a person's identity could be altered, his consumption patterns could be changed. Henry was the only one who fully grasped the potential of the idea. He experimented with a myriad of influencers until he was convinced he could alter a person's perception of self to the point that he could compel them to buy a specific product.

He not only understood the drives that made people acted irrationally. He had learned to control them.

Henry took a sip from the bottle of water on the tray next to his chair. Below, the traffic had died down to the relative quiet of a weekday evening. A siren sounded in the distance, then slowly faded away.

For years Sociologists had explored influencers on social behavior. Efforts to marry these studies with business applications were a dime a dozen. In the eyes of one Professor on the thesis committee, Henry was ". . . aspiring to become just another social scientist attempting to turn a quick buck as a business guru."

To win over the Professor, Henry diluted his thesis. Henry's revision instead focused on the more constructive aspects of consumption patterns. He would save the money-making version for a different audience, those who would appreciate it . . . and pay for it. The result was that Henry received his PHD albeit with an uncelebrated thesis.

Henry thought the left coast might be more open to his ideas so he went to teach at Berkeley. He was quick to change the culture of his classroom, treating students as nothing more than consumers. Unlike traditional consumers, however, students rarely asked for value in return for their expense. Students wanted to be entertained, not challenged. Students were savvy enough to figure out the shortest and easiest path to a marketable degree – at the cost of learning. Henry played to the market. He delivered lessons high in amusement and asked nothing of his students.

The University Deans were conflicted. On the one hand, they were concerned that Henry would erode their brand as a credible learning institution. On the other, the advent of the internet had given students a greater voice in their educational experience. Henry rose to the level of celebrity as students rated him one of the nation's best educators, giving the reputation of the University a boost. Enrollments increased, tuition rose, and the Deans were happy. Critics charged that Henry's popularity equated to the "dumbing down of higher learning." The University combated these concerns by championing the "democratization of education." The market determined the argument's victor. Henry won.

Henry did more than just amuse his audience, though. He *did* endeavor to teach students as well. Rather than adopt the theoretical collegiate method of teaching however, Henry focused on the practical. He prepared his students to make money. Admittedly, his class didn't bother with ethics, but neither did the free market. Henry's students made millions of dollars. Businesses soon came calling and Henry launched his consulting practice. Success bred success, and Henry's consultancy flourished. His clients rationalized ethics concerns by pointing to their competitor's similar practices. These businesses championed the maximization of shareholder profits as their ultimate moral responsibility. Anything less would be unethical.

So Henry's weakness had become his strength. Once powerless – a victim – he finally had gained control. Henry had risen above his Darwinian disadvantages. He had been proud of that, until today.

He could just make out Alcatraz island in the faint moonlight, huddled in the middle of the bay, the lighthouse casting a pinpoint glow.

He used people. He got to the top by pushing others down, as self-absorbed as either of his parents. And now he was on top. Alone. He feasted on the advantages his celebrity afforded. He enjoyed exotic hobbies. He hunted elephants in Botswana. He sailed his catamaran around the world. He base jumped off of the Sydney Harbour Bridge.

He enjoyed the company of beautiful women. Over time the women became just another hobby, and the hobbies all began to grow tiring. Henry'd thought he was seeking fulfillment, but he knew enough about himself to know now he was really just after validation. Fulfillment would have taken him down a different path; one he was too afraid to take.

But with the one person he cared about ready to leave him, he didn't have a choice. Courage was the only option. Henry focused on Alcatraz as he allowed his conscience to speak to him. The message was clear, unmistakable. He'd become his father.

No.

It was a quiet thought, surprisingly simple. He'd thought that the repudiation of everything he'd ever done with his life would be bigger, more dramatic. Apparently not.

Henry turned his head toward the Golden Gate Bridge. He could see the start of the bridge but the termination was obscured by the fog.

He pulled out his iPhone and opened an email.

To: Cheryl Goodwin
From: Henry Maddox
Subject: Out Of Office

Cheryl,

Please cancel all of my appointments next week. I have to respond to an urgent matter.

I will be unavailable on cell phone. I will call you as soon as I return.

Regards,

Henry

A perfection of means,
and confusion of aims,
seems to be our main problem.

- Albert Einstein

CHAPTER **20**

Cheryl arrived at the consulting office early. She had received Henry's odd email the night before. She'd have a full plate while he was gone. Henry had left suddenly before – to join some billionaire on a yacht or jet to Tahiti or something – but he had always left more details regarding his departures and destinations. This was different. She couldn't help but wonder if it had something to do with yesterday's conversation.

Pressley bounded through the front door with youthful enthusiasm. "Good morning Cheryl!"

"Hey Pressley. You look like you're in a good mood."

"Absolutely! I want to thank you again for letting me help on Laroy's campaign. I've really enjoyed it."

"Do you have enough to keep you busy, or do you need me to schedule something for you?"

"Laroy asked me to do some research for him. He gave me a lead on a company he thinks is tied to online gambling. He wants to see if I can corroborate the information."

"Do you need anything from me?"

"Just a work space. Do you mind if I set up in the conference room?"

"Not at all."

Pressley set up her laptop, accessed the office's wireless network, and was soon skipping from link to link, checking GA bulletin boards and corporate filings.

Laroy's tip had come from Jennifer Bennett, the Facility Manager at New Beginnings. Jennifer recently received a patient who had become addicted to an online gambling site. The addiction had progressed from casual video gaming to an online gambling addiction in a matter of months. She had never seen such an aggressive digression. The patient had had previous problems with gambling and felt he had been deliberately targeted by the video gaming site because of his history.

She uncovered a PDF of the company's corporate structure in an odd corner of the State Government's website. The company didn't have any subsidiaries that were mentioned. She looked through the company's different games. Everything seemed innocent enough. Thanks to her studies with Professor Maddox, she could pick out the different demographics the games were aimed at: young children, tweens, teenagers, college students, singles, marrieds, etc. Pressley clicked on a link that mentioned some of the company's partners. Major retailers were listed but none was a cause for concern.

How would she verify the allegation? Pressley leaned back in her chair.

Thomas would know. She reached for her phone.

"Thomas?"

"Hey Pressley what's going on?"

"Hey, I've got a question for an investigative journalist. Know any?"

"Ha ha. Shoot."

"I have a lead on a story I can't seem to confirm. What would a bloodhound like you do in a situation like this?"

"I'd go to the source."

"Okay . . . I'm going to need a ride."

Pressley and Thomas arrived at New Beginnings the next day. They entered the facility and asked for Jennifer Bennett. A woman carrying a clipboard and wearing a dark pant suit soon appeared in the reception area.

"You must be Pressley."

"Thank you for seeing me Mrs. Bennett. This is my friend Thomas. As I'd mentioned on the phone, I'm working with Laroy Elden, researching destructive business practices. Laroy mentioned you had a patient that we might want to talk to?"

"Yes," Jennifer said, "he's eager to share his story. I don't want to overwhelm him though, so I'd prefer if only you and I met with him. Your friend Thomas will have to wait in the reception area."

"No problem at all," said Thomas.

Pressley reached for Thomas' hand and gave it a squeeze.

"The patient is eighteen years-old," Jennifer said, leading Pressley deeper into the facility, "so he's able to provide his own consent to this interview. However, he's asked to remain anonymous. You can call him Robert."

"That sounds fair enough," Pressley said. "Do you mind if I reference you and New Beginnings in the article?"

"I don't see any dangers in that. We're one of only a few internet addiction centers within the United States. Anyone reading your article would be able to identify us pretty quickly anyway."

"All right, it sounds like I understand the ground rules."

"Okay. I've arranged for you to meet with Robert in one of our therapy rooms." Jennifer said. "I'll be listening in on your conversation to assure Robert and you both feel comfortable. I'll terminate the interview if I feel the topic of discussion begins to annoy Robert in any way. I hope that this experience will be therapeutic for him. We try to encourage our patients to talk through their problems."

Pressley followed Jennifer through the doorway into a fair-sized room with a round table in the middle. Three chairs surrounded the table. Robert was already seated. He had on dark jeans and a gray t-shirt, with black, disheveled hair, penetrating blue eyes, a pallid complexion and two days worth of stubble.

Jennifer introduced Pressley who extended her hand to Robert. Robert stood to shake.

"Robert, thank you again for allowing me to visit with you," Pressley said. "Your story might be important. Would you mind telling me first about your history with gambling?"

"Sure. I've been playing Poker since I was a kid – started playing my brother during commercials. I got pretty good at it. My friends and I used to bet little stuff and I'd regularly take it all cause I'd beat'em so bad. When I was about fifteen, I decided to try it with some real money, so I got online and set up an account in my mom's name. I entered her credit card number into the gambling site and bang within seconds, I was playing against people I'd never met before. It gave me a killer rush."

"Was it pretty easy to set up the account?"

"Absolutely, all you've gotta do is check a box that says you're of legal gambling age and give them a credit card number. The only trick to the whole thing was hiding the charges on my mom's credit card."

"And how'd you do that?"

"I started with a minimum balance on the site. I think it was like fifty dollars or something – it came through with some generic name, Northwest Suppliers or something. My mom never paid attention to the charge, so I put fifty dollars more a month on the account for about four months. Like I said, I was pretty good at Poker, so pretty soon I had a balance on the site of about $1,000. At that point I didn't need to use my mom's credit card anymore. I was playing with other people's money."

"And this went on for how long?"

"About a year."

"You were sixteen years-old?"

"Yeah around there."

"And then what happened?"

"I started to get bored. I wanted to see how much I could grow the pot, so I started to make bigger bets. That's the thing about gambling, you start to lose the excitement after a while. You've gotta increase the stakes to keep things interesting."

"And how much time was gambling taking out of your day?"

"None. I'd do it at night when everyone was asleep. I had a computer in my room so it wasn't a big deal. I did lose a lot of sleep though. It got to the point where I wouldn't sleep at all. I would go to school and sleep in class or just skip class and sleep in my car."

"And that's how you got caught? Your grades began to suffer?"

"Actually, no. I'm a pretty smart guy. High School was pretty easy for me. My grades stayed up there and none of my teachers complained – there were kids at school with a lot worse problems than me, so a kid falling asleep or missing class every once in a while didn't exactly stand out. I was smart enough to never miss the same class twice in a row. Eventually, I forged my mom's signature on notes to excuse myself for different reasons."

"You sound pretty cavalier about this whole thing. Any regrets?"

"Then? No way. It was like a game. I enjoyed living on the edge. Now? Sure. I wished I would've been straight up with people, but I know now that my mind was pretty clouded, you know?"

"So ultimately how did your mother find out?"

"One night, I started playing against this one guy. You don't know these people, only their user names. But this guy was super good. After losing to him for like six hands, I finally beat him. I then upped the stakes."

"You bet your whole balance?"

"More than that. I bet my entire balance plus another ten grand."

"Didn't you know the charge would appear on your mom's card?"

"If I won, it wouldn't matter."

"But you lost."

"Well, yeah."

"And what happened when your mom got her credit card statement?"

"She thought it was a mistake. She called the credit card company and complained."

"And?"

"Yeah, the online casino sent her the entire history of my gambling. She was as mad as I've ever seen her. She wanted to sue the gambling company. She said it was their fault for allowing a minor to gamble. None of these online casinos are in the United States though, and all these countries have different rules on gambling. I guess it's really hard to sue them."

"And once she realized that she had to pay the bill?"

"Then she was mad at me. The money wasn't the biggest thing though. She had a really good job. She was more worried about me and my future. She put me in a gambling addiction support group."

"And when did you get out of the support group?"

"I'm still in it. Once an addict, always an addict."

"Right. So how long had you gone without gambling prior to the relapse?"

"Over a year. But about four months ago I was on a social networking sight. A bunch of my friends invited me to play this online role playing game. At first I turned them down but after a while all I saw on the network were updates about how my friends did this or that in the game. I wanted to see what the big deal was, so I enrolled."

"Did you enjoy the game?"

"It was okay, a little light. I was pretty good at it. I racked up points pretty quickly."

"And how did this game turn you back to gambling."

"That's the interesting part. At first the game had nothing to do with gambling. The game was about being a spy – you got points by discovering clues. Pretty soon though, probably after only about a week, the game put my character in a casino. The scenario asked me to prove how good I was at Poker. No money was involved, only points. I figured that because it was just a stupid video game, it wouldn't matter, so I played a couple hands. I killed it and I got a ton of points."

"What was so important about these points?"

"Well, you could trade points for real stuff, like coupons for smoothies or video rentals. But for me, they restricted how I could use my points. I could only use them in a real online casino. I couldn't spend them on anything else."

"And so you logged into the online casino and spent the points."

"And started racking up a balance again, yeah. Two weeks, and I was right back where I had been."

"Don't tell me you stole your mother's credit card number."

"I did . . . it was a real bummer too because she just started to trust me again. But it was like I needed to make up for lost time. I got totally reckless because I thought that at any time I would get caught and all of the fun would stop. So I charged over twenty thousand dollars on a couple of my mom's different credit cards over that next month. I lost it all."

"Robert, let me ask you this. How did this online game find out about your personal battles with gambling?"

"I wondered about that, because none of my friends ever got sent to a casino in the game. And I'm not sure how they did it, but I've got a theory."

"What's that?"

"Since I used a fake user name and my mom's credit cards on the gambling sites, there's no way they could've connected my social media profile with my gambling addiction. I've also been really careful to not have anything on my social network – in my posts, listed as a hobby, nothing – that says that I like anything to do with gambling. So the only way they could have found out was with tracking software on my computer."

"Tracking software?"

"The game put some sort of cookie on my computer that tracked everywhere I went online and then fed it back to the game's database. This made the game smarter–"

"Wait a minute, so the game was spying on you?"

"Exactly."

"Okay, that's creepy. But if you didn't go to any gambling sites, what made the game think you were a recovering addict?"

"I thought a lot about that. I went back and looked at everything I did online during the week I started playing the role playing game. There was nothing in my browser history – I hadn't been to a gambling website for months. But then I checked my emails."

"Your emails?"

"Yeah, my sponsor from my addiction support group had emailed me exactly one day before the game introduced me to the gambling scenario. In my response, I thanked my sponsor for being there for me. I told him how well I was doing. I wrote him quote 'I could never fight my Poker addiction without you.' That was it!"

"The phrase 'Poker addiction.'"

"The game had to have picked up on that phrase. How else would they have known to put me in a scenario where I was playing Poker instead of, like Blackjack or something?"

"And given you free credits that could only be redeemed by gambling at Poker in an online casino."

"Exactly."

"So you think this tracking software was scanning your computer for certain terms, and then adjusted your gaming experience to exploit your addiction?"

"I'm sure of it."

"And just so I have my facts straight, what is the name of the software company that you think targeted you?"

"Zynthe Gaming.   They're located here in the Bay Area."

That was it. She had them.

———

Henry slowed to make sure he had the right spot, then turned onto the windy road after convincing himself that this road was the only possible option.   His foot feathered the accelerator pedal as his Mercedes G550 SUV scaled the switch backs. He'd been driving for five hours. Based upon his GPS directions, he was almost there. Seeing as how the last ten miles of his journey would be on foot and in uncertain terrain, he couldn't guess when he'd arrive.

Henry was North West of the Bay Area in the Plumas National Forest.   His only prior forays into the Sierra Nevada Mountains had been to "escape" to his vacation home in Lake Tahoe. "Escape" then had meant to trade one form of luxury for another. Not this time.

The GPS was now flashing "unconfirmed route." Henry checked his cell phone. There was no signal. He was now on his own, with a compass, a map, and directions from a man whom he'd never met.

Henry felt the wheels of his Mercedes slip and then bite the icy surface as the car's electronic traction system engaged.   Within ten minutes, the snow had completely covered the road. He could no longer see the lines or the edges, but he forged ahead, reasoning that the flatter topography hid the pavement beneath.

In an instant, a large metal gate appeared in front of him. He slammed on the brakes. The sign on the gate read, "Road Closed."

Henry double checked the directions. Everything looked right. He shut off the motor and opened the door to a cold rush of wind and snow. He slammed the door shut again.

He'd get ready inside the car.

Henry climbed into the back and began to outfit himself for the journey. He took time to make sure each layer of clothing was put on properly. A miscalculation could prove fatal. Within minutes, he was back outside and clipping his boots into snowshoes. He locked the Mercedes, strapped on his backpack, and lowered his goggles as he turned to face the trailhead. His watch read 10:22 a.m. Given the difficult terrain, he would have to hurry if he was to arrive before dark.

One's mind stretched
to a new idea
never goes back
to its original dimensions.

- Oliver Wendell Holmes, Sr.

CHAPTER 21

Pressley grabbed Thomas by the collar with two hands and yanked him close to her. "Thomas, this story's for real."

Pressley had wrenched Thomas' six foot frame to where he was now crouched and within inches of her impassioned, sapphire eyes. Administrators within the New Beginnings facility began to take notice.

"Perhaps we should talk about this outside?" Thomas asked.

"Oh yes, of course." Pressley composed herself. "You'll have to forgive me; this is my first scoop. It really gets your blood pumping."

Thomas grabbed Pressley's hand and led her out of the facility. They both walked around the corner to avoid any unwanted attention.

"Okay, give me the details," he said.

"There's a software company here in the Bay Area, Zynthe Gaming. They're placing tracking software on people's computers and handhelds so they can take advantage of their users. In Robert's case they targeted his gambling addiction but in other cases they might focus on something else."

"Did Robert go on record with the story?"

"Yes. Though, he won't come forward with his real name."

"Okay, you did fine. You're right, this is the real deal."

Pressley's smile faded. "Fine? Why not great?"

"It's just that you really need something more if you want this story to pop."

"What do you mean? I can post it to henrymaddox.com. This is exactly the kind of content Laroy wants."

"But what if you can make it better?"

"How?"

"What if you and I go to Zynthe's headquarters and confront the CEO with these charges?"

"Thomas, that sounds . . . dangerous."

"Pressley, don't forget the journalist's mantra."

"Journalists have a mantra?"

"Have you ever heard of the English writer Edward Bulwer-Lytton?"

"The 'dark and stormy night' guy?"

"Well, yeah, but that's not his most famous phrase. In his play 'Richelieu; Or the Conspiracy' back in 1839, he coined 'the pen is mightier than the sword.'"

"Yes, of course."

"Well if the pen was so mighty, think what Bulwer-Lytton would have said about video."

"You want to record the Zynthe CEO's reaction?"

"There's no more effective journalistic technique than a live reaction. We can then post the video to henrymaddox.com. *Then*, you'd have your story."

Pressley paced in a circle, like a boxer ready to enter the ring. She then stopped. "Okay, let's do this thing."

Pressley and Thomas arrived at Zynthe Gaming in Silicon Valley at four o'clock in the afternoon. Thomas parked his car down the street and they both walked to the Zynthe parking lot.

"Can you access an image of the Zynthe CEO from the web?" Pressley asked.

Thomas performed a quick search on his iPhone. "Got him. His name is Gerald Burke. He's in his fifties. Here's a story that says that he always wears silk, untucked Tommy Bahama shirts to work. It looks like he has brownish, gray hair that's receding at the temples. He's about five feet, ten inches tall and probably weighs around two hundred pounds."

The main entrance of the Zynthe building came into view.

"You're sure you can get video on that phone of yours?" asked Pressley.

"Certain. Though I should probably clear up some memory. You never know how long a clip like this will take."

Thomas scrolled, flipped, and tapped his phone as he deleted photos, apps, and music.

A few visitor designated parking places were located in front of the main entrance to the Zynthe building. It was clear that employees parked in the south parking lot. Pressley and Thomas watched the main entrance to assess traffic patterns. Visitors entered through the main door. A receptionist greeted and then gave each visitor a badge. An employee would then come to the lobby to meet the visitor and escort him into Zynthe's offices.

"The CEO isn't going to leave through the lobby," said Thomas. "He's going to want the shortest distance between him and his car. He also won't want to risk getting tied up with visitors, which means we should go to the south side door."

Thomas and Pressley walked around to the south side of the parking lot. A handful of employees were gathered around the south entrance of the building on their smoke breaks. As the employees reentered the building, they used access cards to unlock the doors.

"Do you have any idea what kind of car Burke drives, Pressley?"

"No, I don't. Normally, I'd say just look for the nicest one, but there are some pretty expensive looking cars in this lot."

"Yeah, lots of German steel here. You'd think these guys were performance racecar drivers or something.

"Let's go over here on the west side behind the bushes. We can keep our eyes on the south doorway from there.

When Burke comes out, we'll still have time to ambush him before he gets to the parking stalls."

"Ambush? You're making me nervous. This isn't combat."

"I love the smell of invasion in the morning. It smells like . . . victory." Thomas put his arm around Pressley and smiled. "Lighten up, this is gonna be fun."

At a little after six o'clock, Gerald Burke pushed the south door open and was greeted by a couple of employees. He made light conversation while he fumbled for his car keys in his pocket.

"Let's go, that's him!" Thomas said.

Thomas and Pressley charged through the bushes and advanced until they were within a couple of feet from Burke.

"We're live," Thomas said.

Pressley wiped her perspiring hands on her jeans. She swallowed hard and summoned as much confidence as she could. "Excuse me, Mr. Burke?"

"Yes?"

"My name is Pressley Hamil, and I was wondering if you could answer a couple of questions for me?"

"I guess it depends on the questions."

"I just came from an addiction center. There's a patient there who alleges your gaming software was smart enough to figure out that he had a gambling addiction. He felt your game then deliberately exposed him to gambling stimuli with the intent of readdicting him for your company's profit."

Pressley ran out of breath at the end of the last sentence. No matter how many times she'd practiced the accusation, she could never get the pauses in the right places.

"Young lady, that sounds like an unfortunate situation. But you understand, I can't respond to allegations where I don't know all of the facts."

"Does your gaming software track your user's behaviors, Mr. Burke?"

"No more than what other social networking companies do. We gather data that allows us to better serve our customers. Now if you'll excuse me, I have to get going."

Burke pressed his remote car key to unlock his car door and turned away from Pressley.

"Say something," Thomas whispered. "Keep the pressure on."

Burke opened his car's door and slid himself onto the two-tone leather, bucket seat.

"Mr. Burke, I'm going public with this young man's story tomorrow. Is there anything you'd like me to include as a formal response from Zynthe?"

"Only that we don't respond to unfounded rumors, Miss. We reserve the right to respond once we have read the story."

Burke backed his Porsche 911 Turbo Cabriolet out of the parking space. The top was down, allowing Thomas to continue to film his expression.

Before he left, Burke turned to them. "Out of curiosity, where do you plan to publish this story of yours? Do you represent a news organization?"

"The story will appear on henrymaddox.com tomorrow, Mr. Burke. It's part of a series we're doing on companies that secretly profit off of destructive practices."

Burke's eyes flashed. "You work for Maddox? You tell Henry Maddox that if you publish that story, I'm taking him down with me! Do you hear me?"

"Loud and clear, sir."

Gerald continued to glare at Pressley, as if he might leap out of the car and take a swing at her. Then Thomas lifted up his phone to where Gerald could now see that he had been filmed during the entire encounter.

Gerald revved his engine, shifted into gear, and sped away.

"What just happened?" Pressley asked.

"I'm not sure. I do know one thing though. We've got your story."

———

Henry's legs were beginning to tremble under the weight of his pack as he approached the shelter. He shed his pack and snowshoes and plowed through a drift to the front door. He turned the knob, lowered his shoulder into the door, and gave it a powerful nudge. The door creaked open. Henry entered and surveyed what would be his residence for six more days.

No running water, only a dry sink for dish washing. Although a small electric stove, heater, and lights were present, they weren't working. There were two cots for sleeping and a vault toilet within fifty feet of the shelter.

"You're crazy!" The man said when Henry had asked to rent the shelter. "That shelter won't open for six more weeks. That rustic retreat will be an icebox if you don't hit the season right. Why don't you wait until late May? The snow will have melted and you could sit out on the lookout and enjoy the views of Honey Lake to the north and Last Chance Creek to the south. If you go now, you could freeze to death or, worse, starve."

"No matter," Henry had said. "I want something primitive, somewhere where I can be alone. And did I mention that I'll pay you ten thousand dollars for the week?"

The price offered apparently made the request a lot less absurd. The man sent Henry directions to the cabin and promised he would snowmobile in to make sure it was unlocked and presentable.

"I don't want you to stock it with any food," Henry had said. "I'll pack all of my own food in. I don't want you to make any special arrangements. I want the shelter as is. If you make any efforts to improve the condition of the cabin – even so much as turn on the gas and electricity – you'll void our agreement. Do you understand?"

The man had agreed but did insist on one accommodation. "You can't pack in water for the week. At least allow me to bring in some jugs for you. I'll insulate the jugs so they won't freeze." And that was the only compromise. Though, now that Maddox could see the reality of the shelter, he had wished that he'd allowed himself some heat.

Henry retrieved his backpack from outside and threw it on top of the wood table in the kitchen. He unpacked his food for the week and stacked it on a shelf. He grabbed a portable propane stove, assembled it, and ignited the flame. Within minutes he would have a hot meal. What would it be, beans or rice?

And the day came
when the risk to remain
tight in a bud
became more painful
than the risk
it took to blossom

- Attributed to Anais Nin
(unverified)

CHAPTER 22

Pressley tried the door at Maddox's office.

"It's locked. Cheryl must have left for the evening."

"Didn't they give you a key?" Thomas asked.

"Yes."

"Well then, they expect you to use it. Come on. Open it up."

"Okay, okay."

Pressley opened the office and turned the lights on.

"I have to admit," Thomas said, "I expected more out of an office space from Henry Maddox."

"Yeah, not exactly a lavish command center, eh? He spends most of his time at his client's offices. No need to impress anyone here."

Pressley led Thomas into the conference room where they both setup their laptops.

"You've already transcribed your interview with Robert from New Beginnings, right?"

"Yes."

"Why don't you format it for the blog while I edit the video?"

"Thomas?"

"Yeah."

"What do you think Burke meant when he said that he was going to take Maddox down with him if we published the story?"

"I don't know. He all of a sudden got really upset when we mentioned Maddox's name, didn't he? Maybe it's because Maddox has a following with investment types around the valley? Maddox's disapproval might affect Zynthe's reputation?"

"Yeah, but Burke initially felt fine about dismissing our story as a mere rumor. Honestly Thomas, we're just a couple of college students. Even if we published this story in the *Wall Street Journal*, a company like Zynthe could easily discredit it. Our source won't step forward, and New Beginnings could be seen as having an ax to grind against online gaming companies. As companies like Zynthe are quick to point out, stimulus addiction isn't even a recognized medical condition. Our story doesn't exactly meet the standard of bulletproof investigative journalism."

"I agree, but you've got to understand something about journalism, especially the online variety. It's not the strength of your evidence but the appeal of your story that matters. Of course, you and I know the story's true, but ultimately that doesn't matter. Didn't you learn anything from Maddox's class? Perception is reality. This video clip of Gerald Burke fuming is as good as an admission of guilt."

"Do you think I should wait to launch this story until I at least clear it with Cheryl?"

"Why? Didn't you tell me that Maddox has you working under Laroy? Didn't Laroy give you the tip about the New Beginnings story? Didn't Cheryl tell you that Maddox has given Laroy free license to publish anything he wants? I can't see where this could possibly come back and bite you."

"Yeah, I guess you're right Thomas."

"I know I'm right Pressley. Now let's post this story and get out of here."

———

Henry placed a foam pad over the cot before spreading out his sleeping bag. The beam of light from his flashlight bounced off of the ceiling as he fumbled through his gear, readying himself for bed. He glanced at the thermometer on the outside of the shelter when he returned from using the facilities. It read five degrees. The wind chill had to drive that into the negative double digits. Henry hoped the worst of the night was behind him. If the temperature continued to fall, staying warm through the night would be his greatest challenge.

His watch read 9:17 p.m. Henry hadn't been to bed this early since middle school. His legs throbbed and his back ached from the hike into the shelter. The whistling wind shook the shelter as he struggled to get comfortable. Now settled in his sleeping bag, Henry had nothing to preoccupy his mind.

And that was why he'd come here . . . to confront what he had become.

Henry was now alone in the darkness. Perhaps the cold wouldn't be his biggest adversary after all.

Come what may . . .

- Shakespeare, "Macbeth"

CHAPTER 23

"I'm sorry Mr. Burke, Henry's not in the office right now."

"When will he be in?"

"I don't know. He left on a sudden, urgent matter a couple of days ago."

"Can't you call him?"

"I've tried. I just get his voice mail."

"Give me his lousy cell number."

"I'm sorry Mr. Burke, I'm under strict orders to never release that number without Henry's permission."

"You tell Henry to call as soon as he gets in. Understand?"

"Yes, Mr. Burke."

"Meanwhile, I want you to pull that article about Zynthe off of your website."

"I'm sorry Mr. Burke. Henry is the only one to have authority to override the editorial control of the website. He has left all content decisions up to a gentleman named Laroy Elden. I cannot interfere with the agreement between Mr. Elden and Henry."

"You do understand that the article on your website is disastrous for both your and my companies."

"I understand Mr. Burke. I'll have Henry give you a call as soon as he steps in the office."

Cheryl hung up the phone and stared at it a moment. Then she shouted, "Pressley, what have you done?"

Pressley popped out of the conference room as if she were waiting for the call. "What's up?"

"I think you know. I just got off the phone with Gerald Burke of Zynthe Gaming. He's dumbfounded as to why we would run such a negative article about his company on our website."

"Why's Gerald Burke so concerned about what we have to say?"

"Zynthe Gaming is one of Henry's clients!"

"Oh no . . ." Pressley collapsed into one of the leather chairs in the reception area. "I had no idea. I'm . . . I'm so sorry Cheryl. That's why he was so angry when we told him we were going to post the story on henrymaddox.com."

"You mean you actually spoke to him before posting the story?"

"Yeah, we wanted to get his reaction. There's even video."

Cheryl spun to her computer and called up henrymaddox.com. The headline on the landing page read "Zynthe Gaming Addicts Users for Profit." A video image was placed directly under the headline. Cheryl clicked on it.

The video showed Pressley approaching Gerald Burke in a parking lot.

"I just came from an addiction center. There's a patient there who alleges your gaming software was smart enough to figure out that he had a gambling addiction. He felt your game then deliberately exposed him to gambling stimuli with the intent of readdicting him for your company's profit."

Cheryl watched the interview unfold, with Burke remaining pleasantly, professionally evasive. Occasional text appeared at the bottom of the screen, identifying Burke and his car – a Porsche 911 that started at $149,000. Then came the end, when Burke's professional demeanor suddenly slipped.

"You tell Henry Maddox that if you publish that story, I'm taking him down with me! Do you hear me?"

The camera jostled, steadied, and then zoomed in close to Burke's impassioned face. The shot held tight on Burke until he looked directly at the camera. Burke's eye contact with the camera revealed sudden discomfort. Burke then sped away. Text appeared at the end of the video: "'Destruction is not profit.' – Frederic Bastiat (1850)"

Immediately below the video embed was the text of an interview with the kid from New Beginnings. Cheryl scanned it quickly. Oddly, she found she was smiling by the end.

"Well, I can certainly see why Burke is so upset," said Cheryl. "His reaction makes him look awfully defensive, not to mention really unlikeable. Once viewers learn that Zynthe is a client of Henry's, they'll presume the information has to be accurate – it is, isn't it?"

"I trust it."

"All right. So Zynthe Gaming is in for a public relations nightmare. This is going to be disastrous for us as well Pressley. Henry's consulting practice relies on absolute privacy. Once Henry's other clients realize that henrymaddox.com sold out Burke, we're going to get calls from Henry's clients and their teams of lawyers. And Zynthe is peanuts compared to some of Henry's other clients. This could mean the end of Henry's entire consulting practice."

"Oh my . . . I'm so sorry Cheryl. I'll take the post down immediately–"

"No!"

"Excuse me?"

"You can't take down that post, Pressley. Only Laroy can authorize the take down of the post. Henry and Laroy had an agreement that Laroy would have sole control over the content of henrymaddox.com. This isn't our call. We need to speak to Laroy, immediately."

Laroy arrived at Maddox's office that afternoon. "I came here as soon as I got your call. What's this emergency?"

"I'm so sorry Mr. Elden," Pressley said. "I did as you asked. I researched the story at New Beginnings and I followed all of the leads. I just didn't know it would turn out like this."

"Like what?"

"Mr. Elden, have you seen the lead story on henrymaddox.com today?" Cheryl asked.

"First thing this morning. I thought it was wonderful – a perfect example of a company profiting off of other people's suffering. Excellent job, Pressley."

"Well sir," Cheryl said. "Therein lies the problem. Zynthe Gaming is actually a client of Henry's. Of course neither you nor Pressley knew this when you uncovered this story. But now that you do know, you can certainly appreciate the difficult position both Zynthe and our consultancy are in right now."

"I see," Laroy said. "Zynthe thinks that Pressley was acting on inside information – that somehow Henry tipped her off with the intention of compromising Mr. Burke."

"Exactly. And this puts Henry's entire consultancy at risk."

"I should say so," said Laroy. "Henry makes his living teaching companies these types of exploitative techniques. If Henry gave up Zynthe, what company will he give up next?"

"So you understand our predicament." Cheryl said.

"I certainly do. What does Henry say about this?"

"That's another problem. He's out of town for the week and we can't reach him."

"And since Henry and I have an agreement, you want to see if I can make an exception and retract the Zynthe post."

"That's right."

"What do the current site statistics on henrymaddox.com look like?" Laroy asked.

"The Zynthe post is going viral," Cheryl said. "Zynthe is the fastest growing video gaming company in the world. Our traffic is up 400 percent and climbing. Other news organizations and blogs are linking to our site. If we want to kill the story, we need to do it now. We can still recover from this."

"And what if we wait?" Laroy asked.

"Other websites will want to cash in on the momentum by mirroring the information. As people search for the Zynthe story, they could be directed to all sorts of copycat sites. It'll be impossible to retract what we've written. We'll no longer have control of the story."

"And this will take how long?"

"It depends on the momentum of the story. Based on what I'm seeing, we probably have less than twenty four hours."

"So we can still save this mess."

Cheryl exhaled. "Yes sir, I knew that you'd understand."

"Okay, take down the post Cheryl. Although it pains me to say that after Pressley did such a fantastic job. I want this story to come to light but not at the expense of you or Pressley."

"Thank you Mr. Elden." Pressley threw her arms around Laroy.

Laroy walked toward the door and then stopped midway. He turned and looked back at Cheryl. "I wouldn't get too comfortable though. Secrets seem to always have a way of getting out. Zynthe and Henry may have skirted today's mess. That doesn't mean their actions will go without consequence."

Pressley and Cheryl were silent.

————

Henry sat in a hard, wooden chair atop the lookout deck. The sudden warmth was unexpected, considering the prior day's storm. The melting snow created a rhythmic patter as it poured from rain gutters onto the concrete patio below. Henry had removed his jacket and gloves. For the first time in five days, he considered himself comfortable. He had grown used to the solitude. He no longer fought his thoughts. He allowed them to distill on his mind. His pride yielded to humility. His fear gave way to curiosity. What if he could still change the course of his life?

Henry's watch read 12:24 p.m. He had been reading for five hours, only the last two of which had been outdoors. He was almost at the end of the now underlined, annotated, and highlighted tome – *The Brothers Karamazov*. Margaret Elden's brief promotion of the book and its author had affected Henry. The imprisoned solitude within Dostoevsky's life had led to introspection and philosophical change. It was this idea that had led Henry to the mountains. It was the reading of Dostoevsky's novel, however, that he hoped would instill the temerity for his own sustained change.

Henry needed a foundation for a new life, something he could rely upon for structure and support. His pursuit was for knowledge that had been tested, torqued, and twisted and still remained. He sought the morality, humanity and wisdom that had survived the whims of fashion. Henry saw in Dostoevsky a fellow traveler who had arrived at where he aspired to go. Dostoevsky's 700 page, eight point font opus didn't disappoint.

Henry had now numbered the highlighted passages within the novel. Although published in the nineteenth century and set in Russia, Dostoevsky's writing fit with current American culture. The problems Dostoevsky addressed were human problems that transcended time and country. The book spoke to Henry in a direct, uncompromising, and intelligent way. Dostoevsky had become Henry's anchor.

"The world says: 'You have needs – satisfy them. You have as much right as the rich and the mighty. Don't hesitate to satisfy your needs; indeed, expand your needs and demand more.' This is the worldly doctrine of today. And they believe that this is freedom. The result for the rich is isolation and suicide, for the poor, envy and murder; for while the poor have been handed all these rights, they have not been given the means to enjoy them."

Henry reflected on how his theories enslaved the ignorant by promoting pointless consumption. He had spent his life turning people into puppets that could be controlled by business interests.

> "Some claim that the world is gradually becoming united, that it will grow into a brotherly community as distances shrink and ideas are transmitted through the air. Alas, you must not believe that men can be united in this way. To consider freedom as directly dependent on the number of man's requirements and the extent of their immediate satisfaction shows a twisted understanding of human nature, for such an interpretation only breeds in men a multitude of senseless, stupid desires and habits and endless preposterous inventions. People are more and more moved by envy now, by the desire to satisfy their material greed, and by vanity."

Henry had returned to this passage multiple times since reading it. He again checked the book's initial date of publication – 1879 and 1880. This insight was written before air travel, before automobiles, before telephones, before radio, before television, or before any modern transportation or communication device of any significance. At that time, he was probably only considering railways, steam ships, and the telegraph. And yet Dostoevsky refuted the prevalent argument of today – that a "brotherly community" could be formed by shrinking distances and ideas being transmitted through the air. Dostoevsky's argument was as applicable in the internet age as it was in the age of steam. What did social media and video gaming companies do but spawn ". . . a multitude of senseless, stupid desires and endless preposterous inventions." Technology had provided miraculous improvement to the quality of life, but he had used these inventions to fragment the sense of community? Henry thought of Benjamin at New Beginnings and his gaming addiction. Benjamin had grown alone, apart, and out-of-touch . . . the opposite of community.

Henry thumbed through the pages.

> "That is why the idea of service to mankind and brotherly love has been dying out in the world; indeed, now it is often sneered at, for what can a man do who has become the slave of the innumerable needs and habits he has invented for himself? He lives in his separate little world and does not care about the great world outside. The result of all this is that, today, when more material goods have been accumulated than ever, there is less joy."

The notion of "material goods" in Dostoevsky's age paled in comparison to today. In contemporary society, possessions controlled their owners. Certainly this was Benjamin's experience – as well as countless others. When Laroy had first come to him, he'd said two things that were absolutely true. The content of his message was spot-on. And nobody cared. Laroy had trusted Henry to get the message out. Laroy knew it would take a different kind of messenger to be heard above consuming, frivolous distractions. He had not given Laroy his best, not even close. If Henry's life was to find meaning, this would be his purpose.

Henry turned to a fourth highlighted quote:

"Stupidity is brief and straightforward, while intelligence is tortuous and sneaky. Intelligence is crooked, while stupidity is honest. I've carried my argument to the point of despair, and the more stupidly I present it, the more to my advantage that will be."

Henry had manipulated the naive to enrich the savvy. Now the time had come to be direct and unmistakable . . . honest and forthright. Henry hoped his sabbatical had prepared him for the pending onslaught of criticism. When he turned against the interests he once promoted, his former friends would label him a fool and his clients would do everything possible to discredit him. He had to be prepared. With limitless power and untold wealth at stake, corporate interests wouldn't stop at mere name calling. No measures would be considered too extreme to silence Henry Maddox.

What mean ye
that ye beat my people to pieces,
and grind the faces of the poor?

- Isaiah 3:15 (KJV)

CHAPTER 24

For the first time he could remember, Henry slept well in his San Francisco home. Although his face was chapped and burned by the exposure of the prior week, he looked rested, at peace as he entered the door of his office.

"Good morning Cheryl. How was your week?"

Cheryl was frantically clicking from link to link on her computer, apparently too busy to welcome Henry back with the fanfare that he'd hoped. "You couldn't have picked a better time to disappear boss." Cheryl raised her eyes from her screen just long enough for Henry to feel her icy stare.

"Ouch. So . . . not good?"

Cheryl came at Henry. "You have no idea what your absence has put us through. We had no way to get hold of you. We didn't know where you were or when you'd get back."

"Okay. It'll be okay. What happened?"

At the sound of voices, Pressley appeared at the doorway of the filing room. "Professor Maddox, it was my fault."

"What was your fault? Did somebody die or something? Why are you both so hysterical?"

"I followed a lead that Laroy Elden gave me for his 'Destruction Is Not Profit' campaign. It led me to New Beginnings and then to Zynthe Gaming. I honestly didn't know Gerald Burke was your client." Pressley's body shook and her voice started to crack. "I'm just so, so sorry."

"Pressley come over here and sit down. Please relax. There's nothing you've done that can't be undone."

Pressley sank down in one of the client chairs in the reception area. "But there's more sir. I brought a friend who captured the entire confrontation with Mr. Burke on video. When we told Mr. Burke we were from henrymaddox.com, he flipped out. We posted the video to Laroy's campaign–"

"Gerald Burke called in a tirade and ordered us to take the video down," Cheryl said. "I told him we didn't have the authority to make that call and that you were out of town. You remember your agreement with Laroy was that he had full control over the henrymaddox.com content?"

"That's right."

"Well, Pressley and I wanted to honor that agreement so we called Laroy and asked him for permission to remove the video."

"And what did Laroy say?"

"He agreed to take it down."

"Okay, so we sustained some minor harm, right? Some people saw the video but now no one can find it to verify its existence. This stuff happens all the time. It'll blow over in a couple of days."

"It's not quite that simple," Cheryl said. "Before we could take down the video Harmony Winter grabbed it. So even though it's not on henrymaddox.com, she made sure it was all over the internet."

"Winter, that gal is unbelievable!" Henry caught himself before putting his fist through the drywall. "But I probably would have done the same thing." He whispered. "How long has the video been out there?"

"For an entire week."

"Okay. What do the numbers look like?"

"Henry, it's really bad. Mirror sites all over the web now have the video. There's no way to undo this thing. Everyone is referring to the incident as being 'burked.' Just when we thought the incident had played out, celebrities have spontaneously tweeted about the video or referenced a 'Burke moment.' Henry, we can't–"

"What are the numbers, Cheryl?"

"The traffic spiked the day after the video was posted. Users hit henrymaddox.com looking for more context. We reached 50 million hits–"

"50 million! I don't think Huffington Post draws those numbers."

"Yeah, I know. It's settled down a bit. We've been trending at about 20 million hits a day since."

"And our servers have been able to handle the loads?"

"I was afraid that if henrymaddox.com went down, it would compromise your agreement with Laroy. So I asked our data center to give us more boxes. They kept us from shutting down. They're now asking for permission to issue a press release saying how pleased we were that they responded so quickly. They, like everyone else want to leverage the publicity."

"This is extraordinary. How many users have signed up for Laroy's campaigns?"

"Over 5 million users. All of these users are also subscribed to the henrymaddox twitter feeds. You now are ranked in the top 50 of twitterers."

"Twitterers, huh? I didn't even know that was a word."

"It may not be, but you get the picture."

"So what's Gerald's response been?"

"You'll appreciate this. He now has an equivalent number of twitter followers. His last tweet, as of yesterday was: 'Henry Maddox will set this straight when he returns from wherever he is #truthbetold #zynthe.'"

"I take it he wants to see me immediately?"

Cheryl offered a wry smile. "Ya think, Henry?"

"Okay, Cheryl tell Gerald I'm on my way to see him and that I'll explain everything to him when I get there."

"What are you going to tell him?" Pressley's voice was still quivering.

"The truth."

Henry stood in Gerald Burke's office inspecting his memorabilia while Gerald wrapped up a meeting in Zynthe's conference room. It was apparent that Gerald had grown accustomed to his newfound wealth and prestige.

Photographs of Gerald at political and charity fundraisers papered the walls, along with shots of Gerald playing golf with Tiger Woods at Augusta National and of him backstage with Bono at a U2 concert. The intended impression was clear; Gerald Burke was a big deal.

Henry was looking at a photo of Gerald being interviewed by Maria Bartiromo on the financial news when the man himself entered the room.

"What kind of person leaves control of his business to a half-witted college intern and then disappears?" he said without preamble. "I've had to grovel in front of my investors to maintain control here at Zynthe. We've lost half our customers. Half, Henry! Do you know how long it took us to get to our former customer base?"

"Yes. Well, I suppose I owe you an explanation—"

"You owe me a whole lot more than that Henry." Suddenly, Gerald sagged. "You've put me through one of the most harrowing experiences of my life. I've given our response quite a bit of consideration, and the good news is that I have a plan." Gerald sat down at his desk and grabbed a legal pad that was covered with scribbles. His voice became subdued. "First, you can issue a statement affirming Zynthe's practices as among the most ethical in the business; that our privacy policies exceed industry standards, etc. Second, you can talk about how the posted video was unfairly edited and outside the full context of the real conversation between me and the young lady. Third, you can say how you've since dismissed the young lady from your company because she exhibited malicious intent in coming after me in such an injurious manner."

Still standing, Henry walked to Gerald's office window. "I suppose that would be big of you."

"I'm looking after our mutual interests, Henry. You started this absurd campaign for who knows what reason. Regardless, it's now time to end it. You and I have too much at stake."

Henry ran his index finger over a glass encased, Michael Jordan autographed basketball. "You're saying that if I scapegoat the young lady and come to your defense, all will then return to normal?"

"Well, we may have an opportunity to spin things to our favor, maybe show how this was a brilliant publicity stunt. Look, you and I both now have over five million twitter followers. That in itself is pretty remarkable."

"Maybe we can leverage the attention to promote one of your new video games? Do you have any games having to do with investigative journalism? Or *any* combative relationship even–"

"Yes! There you go Henry. That's the type of thinking we need. I knew two smart guys like us could turn this mess into an opportunity."

"There's only one problem Gerald."

"And what's that?"

"I quit."

"You . . . quit what?"

"Exploiting people."

"Henry, what are you talking about? Who are we exploiting?"

"The weak, the naive, the unsuspecting, the uneducated, the undisciplined–"

"You're talking about Zynthe's customers."

Henry approached Gerald's desk. "To be fair to you, I'm talking about everything I've done over the course of my entire career. This is much larger than you or Zynthe. I need to save you from what I've become. If I don't take a stand now, it will be too late. Gerald, make Zynthe into a good company. It doesn't have to be great. You can make a comfortable living without using the approaches I suggested in our strategy sessions. You don't need to be rich at the expense of others. Believe me, it costs too much in the end."

"Henry, I have four hundred employees in this building alone that expect a paycheck every week. By the end of the year, our plan calls for double that number. Investment bankers have bet millions on me. They need a return on their investment. I have revenue numbers that I have to hit so that we can stay on track to go public."

"It's not worth it Gerald. Trust me, you'll only get in deeper. Don't ignore your conscience. It won't go away."

"You don't get it Henry!" Gerald grabbed an autographed baseball from a decorative display on his desk and threw it across the room. The ball shattered the Maria Bartiromo photograph. "Too many people rely on me – on you. We don't have the luxury of having a conscience. That's the price we pay for doing what we do."

"That's why I'm not doing it any more. I'm sorry."

"What does that mean, 'I'm sorry?'"

"I'm done with this whole charade. The only way out for me now is to educate others. Don't worry, I won't reveal proprietary secrets. But I'm going to pull back the curtain. It's the only chance I have at redemption."

Gerald leaned forward and rested his elbows on his desk. His voice became quiet and harsh.

"You do that Henry and you won't just have me to fight. You know this, right? I'll go to all your clients. We'll band together. We'll humiliate you. We'll marginalize you. Henry, we will ruin you. And you know perfectly well what we can do."

"Believe me, I understand the consequences. And you know what? I don't really care. I'm done with being muddle-headed."

"Muddle-headed?"

"Yes muddle-headed in a way that has allowed me to spend my life pulling off all sorts of shady little financial deals and not much else. That's Dostoevsky."

Henry stood up and walked out of Gerald's office.

"Oh and so now you've found enlightenment?" Gerald's shout from behind him awoke a throng of Zynthe employees from their programming trances. They peeked over their cubicles to watch Henry walk down the hall and enter the elevator. "You'll regret this day Maddox!"

But Henry was smiling. Only ten o'clock, and it was already a good day.

. . . that widows
may be their prey,
and that they may rob
the fatherless!

- Isaiah 10:2. (KJV)

CHAPTER 25

"I appreciate all of you making yourselves available for this conference call. My name is Gerald Burke, I'm Chief Executive Officer of Zynthe Gaming. As you all know by now, my business has been compromised by a once trusted friend, Henry Maddox. I finally met with Henry yesterday in my office. He's been out-of-town during this whole fiasco, which in and of itself was unforgivable. Despite my anger, though, I was willing to forgive him. Knowing Henry's remarkable gifts, as you all do, I was certain he would have a way to creatively spin this public relations debacle to a positive. I even approached him with some suggestions.

"Henry was not only unwilling to work with me, he told me that he was no longer in the business of, as he called it, 'profiting at other people's expense.' But that alone is not why I called you. Henry Maddox is not content to leave quietly. He said that he feels his only path to redemption is to expose the so called wrongs he's committed."

There were some quiet murmurs and a couple of gasps from the other participants in the conference call.

"Now I'm sure you understand what this means for each of your companies," Gerald said, "but allow me to detail some of my concerns. Each of us has been involved in confidential strategy sessions with Henry. He's convinced me and I assume most of you that the only way to get ahead of your competition is by pushing boundaries. Not that what we do isn't perfectly legal. We all have an army of attorneys that assures we're on the right side of the law. What I'm concerned about is a trial in the court of public opinion. How will each of us fare when all of our dirty laundry is aired by one of the henrymaddox.com campaigns?

"Those of us who have had the unfortunate experience of having gone through a divorce may understand how ugly this type of thing can get. When a once trusted partner decides to disclose your most intimate secrets with the intent of destroying you, there is no end to the viciousness. Maddox's attacks will be worse. His assaults will be directed at each of us as business leaders. The harm, however, will be felt by not only us but also by our families, our employees, and our investors. I ask of each of you: who has the stronger moral compass? Henry Maddox as he destroys lives to calm a troubled conscience, or each of us who battles not for ourselves but for the countless people who look to us for their livelihood? Maddox is a traitor. We protect those loyal to us.

"But now for the good news, I had no idea how deep and far reaching Maddox's client list was until I assembled each of you. We have over one hundred companies and all of the major industry groups represented on this call. Collectively, we can discredit any of Maddox's accusations. We have multimedia conglomerates that can use their voices through print and online media, television, radio, and even entertainment to frame and dominate our case against him. We have well respected business icons on this call whose voices carry significantly more weight than a disgruntled former consultant.

"Make no mistake, collectively we will triumph. The loser in this exercise will be Henry. Our key to victory, however, must hinge on our collective commitment and coordination. To this end, I've volunteered to lead the cause. As you can imagine, this is personal."

———

Henry, Cheryl, and Pressley were seated around the dining room table at Laroy's home. Laroy was at the head. Margaret had just brought in a tray of oatmeal cookies.

"Laroy, Margaret . . ." Henry looked them both directly in the eyes. "I owe you an apology. I agreed to the henrymaddox.com campaigns as an experiment. The truth of it though is that I never intended to have an honest contest of ideas. I just wanted access to your followers. I wanted to better understand their psychologies so that I could figure out how to market to them . . . no, to exploit them. Without your knowledge, I'd created my own campaigns to fragment people like you – committed, procommunity people."

"We know," Laroy said.

"You . . . how long?"

"Margaret picked it up," Laroy said.

"What can I say," she said. "I've raised teenagers. You're a pretty good liar, but not that good."

"Okay. Anyway, I viewed people like you as out-of-touch. You believe you can change the world for good, one person at a time. You prioritize your children and your neighbors above your own consumption. Fulfillment for you comes through love and service, not accumulation of material goods. I'd thought these ideas placed people like you in an emotionally vulnerable position. You strive for an ideal, and since people are inherently imperfect, they will ultimately let you down. You would argue of course that it's more satisfying to strive for improvement than to give up on others. But if I could overwhelm people like you and blur the belief in an intrinsic self worth, I knew I would be able to manipulate you. As Dostoevsky put it in The Brothers Karamazov: '. . . if there was any natural law, it was precisely this: Destroy a man's belief in immortality and not only will his ability to love wither away within him but, along with it, the force that impels him to continue his existence on earth. Moreover, nothing would be immoral then, everything would be permitted . . .'"

Margaret raised her eyebrows and gave Henry an approving nod.

"Once people are distracted enough, they don't have to give thought to the divine or pay attention to how their behavior affects others. They are without moorings and easily manipulated. And so I started to see success in my sample size – your people."

"How?" Laroy asked.

"It wasn't hard. I established a social network. Procommunity people enjoyed the collaboration of my online community, it was a natural transition. Once I got them online, I obscured the idea of intrinsic self worth by encouraging comparisons with other people – people who were unnaturally perfect because I'd made them up. I appealed to peoples' egos as well as their insecurities by promoting the idea that it was not enough to be unique or to do good. My intent was to convince them that the only meaningful accomplishment was to be *better* than someone else. That got them more concerned with promoting a perception of goodness than with actually doing good. In other words, I gave them a short cut. They didn't need to achieve some sense of inner peace, or experience a confirmation from some higher being to feel validated. All they needed to do was be better than their virtual friends . . . and they could even lie about how good they were. Competition and comparisons drove sales in products and services that gave one person an edge over another. And then I had them. These users had abandoned the only true source of contentment, and now they would never be at peace.

"I had proven that even people with so called self respect could be compromised. I had discovered a winning formula. I felt an extraordinary sense of accomplishment. And then . . . I realized I was in the same boat as my victims.

I'd discovered powerful forms of persuasion. I'd made unspeakable amounts of money. And yet, I was miserable. I could not be sated. I was lost.

"And so after Cheryl confronted me and gave me an ultimatum, I retreated to the mountains. I needed to go to a place where there were no distractions. I needed to prove to myself that I could subsist on the most limited of possessions. I needed to see if I had the courage to do what it was going to take to finally find meaning in my life."

"With the help of Dostoevsky," Margaret said.

"Absolutely. So my purpose for calling you here today is to ask your forgiveness and commit to you that I'll do better. From now on, I will dedicate my undivided attention to promoting and expanding Laroy's campaign."

Laroy stood and approached Henry. He rested his hand on Henry's shoulder.

"Henry I can't speak for Pressley, Cheryl or even Margaret, but I forgive you. Your future is brighter than your past."

Henry stood up and embraced Laroy. One by one Cheryl, Pressley, and Margaret all joined the embrace.

"Well there you have it Henry," Laroy said. "It looks like we're all of one mind on this."

"I appreciate your willingness to give me a second chance," Henry said. "But now to practical details. Although Laroy's campaigns have attracted tremendous interest, the mere fact that I've been involved up until now has given the opposition a sense of security. I'd assured my clients I wouldn't allow Laroy's cause to grow too quickly or make much of a difference. Now that I'm on Laroy's side, my clients have no such assurance.

"We're battling powerful interests who've staked billions of dollars on deceptive strategies. They know I can singlehandedly bring them to their knees. They won't let that happen. I'm confident their play will be to come after me personally. I know this because this is exactly what I'd advise them to do. So this is going to get ugly. I need each of you to fade into the background for a bit. There's no reason to give the opposition more than one target. I caused these problems. Let me take the hits."

"That's your call," Laroy said.

"And now I need to ask Margaret a favor. I apologize for not asking you this in advance, but I felt you needed to hear my admissions first. Margaret, your introduction to Dostoevsky got me started on this road. Could you inspire us with another literary reference for our cause?"

"I think I can find something that might apply Henry."

Margaret arose from her chair, left the dining room, and then returned with two large books.

"Let's see if we have any literary scholars in the room. Can anyone here tell me who penned the following lines?"

"It was the middle of a bright tropical afternoon that we made good our escape from the bay. The vessel we sought lay with her main-topsail aback about a league from the land and was the only object that broke the broad expanse of the ocean."

Margaret looked around at the blank faces within the room. "No one? How about this one?" Margaret opened the second book.

"Call me Ishmael. Some years ago – never mind how long precisely – having little or no money in my purse, and nothing particular to interest me on shore, I thought I would sail about a little and see the watery part of the world. It is a way I have of driving off the spleen and regulating the circulation. Whenever I find myself growing grim about the mouth; whenever it is a damp, drizzly November in my soul; whenever I find myself involuntarily pausing before coffin warehouses, and bringing up the rear of every funeral I meet– "

"*Moby Dick* by Melville," Pressley said.

"That's it, Pressley. *Moby Dick* is considered by many to be one of the greatest literary works of all time. But would it surprise you to know that the first selection was the beginning of another nineteenth century seafaring novel named *Omoo*, by the same author, Herman Melville?"

"I wasn't aware that Melville had written other works," Laroy said.

"The first passage I cited doesn't sound much like the Melville we remember, does it? The writing is good but doesn't quite carry the same punch as *Moby Dick*. Why? It's something literary critics call 'voice.' *Omoo* was published in 1847, four years before *Moby Dick*. The greatest voices develop with experience. These voices convey credibility and inspire confidence. The opening of *Moby Dick* is one of the most recognizable passages in literature, but it took multiple published attempts to arrive at that commanding language."

"That's fascinating Margaret," Henry said, "but I don't see how it applies here."

"Henry, your life up to this point can be viewed as nothing more than preparation. Now, you're about to find your voice."

A good catchword
can obscure analysis
for fifty years.

- Wendell L. Wilkie

CHAPTER 26

In the morning, five million followers of henrymaddox.com got the following tweet:

> Henry Maddox is back. Hear what he has to say re: the Gerald Burke/Zynthe Gaming revelations. henrymaddox.com #destructionisnotprofit.

The landing page of henrymaddox.com displayed the following:

> While I was unreachable, the "Destruction Is Not Profit" campaigns launched by Laroy Elden uncovered startling revelations about some of Zynthe Gaming's business practices. Specifically, the games made by Zynthe monitor their user's online behavior, even when the games are not being played. The intent is for Zynthe to profit off of the data they assemble. But this is not all. The claims further assert that Zynthe gained access to a specific user's personal information

that identified him as a recovering online gambling addict, and that Zynthe then used this information to introduce the user to an online gambling site. Zynthe even gave the user free credits for poker, which was the addict's prior game of choice, to entice him to play a couple of free hands. The story goes on to suggest that as a consequence of Zynthe's data collection practices, this individual relapsed into gambling, lost tens of thousands of dollars, and now resides in a rehabilitation center for recovering addicts.

Speculation has surrounded these allegations for over a week. Gerald Burke, Chief Executive Officer of Zynthe Gaming, claims that this story has been manufactured by Laroy Elden to promote his "battle against capitalism." Laroy Elden and Gerald Burke have awaited my return as both feel that I am the only person qualified to settle this dispute.

So where do I stand? About one year ago I met with Gerald Burke to discuss growth strategies for the then struggling company, Zynthe Gaming. I convinced Gerald that if he really wanted to grow the company, he needed to employ a more aggressive strategy. The strategy I recommended to him – and that he accepted – was to track their user's behaviors, assemble the data, and convert it to profit. In particular I shared with him how he could use his gaming system as a gateway drug to more addictive stimuli such as online gambling and pornography. Zynthe would then derive ambiguous "partner revenues" off of these introductions.

Long story short, Laroy Elden's accusations against Zynthe are true.

I understand that this disclosure damages Zynthe's reputation and causes many of the diligent, unsuspecting workers at Zynthe to suffer. For this, I am truly sorry. My admission also implicates me. I have destroyed others for profit.

I first agreed to host Laroy Elden's "Destruction Is Not Profit" campaign with the stated goal of conducting an experiment. Little did I know at the time that I was the test subject. Laroy Elden has shown me that I was wrong. I am now convinced that if a vibrant, productive capitalism is to survive, virtue must temper self-interest.

My admission therefore is not only that I collaborated with Zynthe to employ destructive practices. I have also done the same for hundreds of other companies in most all major industries. In the coming days I will release the names of these clients and the destructive practices they have employed for their own financial gain. I appeal to you as activists and consumers to boycott these companies until they commit to right the wrongs they have committed.

With Regret,

Henry Maddox

Within an hour, Henry's admission had gone viral. The data center hosting the henrymaddox.com website racked multiple new servers to handle the anticipated traffic spikes. Henry's letter had stolen the news cycle.

By noon, Henry had arrived at his office and found both Pressley and Cheryl watching news snippets on the internet. Cheryl was shouting at one of the commentators when Henry interrupted.

"You do know that she can't hear you," he said.

"Makes me feel better anyway. You wouldn't believe what these people are saying about you. You need to defend yourself."

"No, I really don't. This is all part of the process. We've gotten my admission into the public conscience. My words stand on their own."

"But all of the cable news outlets are saying this is a publicity stunt. They say you're promoting yourself by debasing a good company like Zynthe. All of these shows are hosting Gerald Burke and they're throwing him softballs!"

"Sure. Every one of these media companies is owned by a major corporation, most of whom used to be my clients. They're working with Gerald to spin the story. It's classic propaganda – they're using their bully pulpit to discredit me before I expose them."

"Well," Cheryl said, "watch this interview and see if you still feel philosophical about all of this."

Moderator: "Thank you Mr. Burke for coming on our show. I realize this past week has been pretty exhausting for you."

Burke: "I appreciate the opportunity to clear my name."

Moderator: "We should mention that we extended an offer for Mr. Maddox to come on our show but our calls to him were not returned."

Burke: "I can't say that I'm surprised."

Cheryl paused the interview. "You know, they never contacted us."

"I wouldn't go on those shows anyway," Henry said. "Even though they can't control what I say, they can edit the contents of any interview to say what they want it to say."

Cheryl unpaused the interview.

Moderator: "What do you mean by that comment Mr. Burke?"

Burke: "Only that if Henry Maddox had a defensible position, he would be here to defend it."

Moderator: "Why would a man like Henry Maddox not only agree with the allegations set forth by

Laroy Elden's now infamous campaigns but also implicate himself in his admissions?"

Burke: "First of all, it's important to understand who Laroy Elden is. All you need to do is read some of Elden's profamily speeches to see what type of a right wing nut job he is. He's chauvinistic, homophobic, absolutely unrealistic as to sexual morality . . . and on top of all of that, he's a conspiracy theorist that thinks corporations want to steal your children. Do we really want to take this guy seriously?"

"That's not true!" shouted Pressley. "Children get lost in these arguments. Laroy's just giving them a voice."

"That was a talking point Pressley," Henry said. "It distracts from the issue, which is that Zynthe as well as other companies want to break apart the traditional family. You know very well from class that once the family is fragmented, the demand for other services and products increase. This provides the new market opportunity."

Cheryl again resumed the interview.

Moderator: "So Mr. Elden's motive is to take down companies like Zynthe that support more inclusive lifestyles. Is that correct?"

Burke: "That's correct. It's no secret that we've been very active in supporting social causes that promote progressive lifestyles."

Moderator: "What then would be the motive for Mr. Maddox?"

Burke: "Maddox is an opportunist. He has often said so publicly. What he saw was an opportunity to use Elden's campaigns to improve his position with Zynthe. A couple of days ago, Maddox and I met in my office. He had waited to take a position on this whole fiasco to increase his leverage with me. He wanted to see me squirm. I have to admit, it was a very uncomfortable time for me. So when I met with him, I asked him to set things straight, to tell the truth."

Moderator: "And what was Mr. Maddox's response."

Burke: "He told me he would publicly support my position if I gave him stock in Zynthe."

Moderator: "He asked you for compensation in exchange for his loyalty?"

Burke: "It had nothing to do with loyalty. He wanted me to pay him for telling the truth."

Moderator: "Which is?"

Burke: "That this whole story is a fabrication."

Moderator: "But it is a point of record that Henry Maddox had consulted with your company. He even tweeted after one of his meetings with you, 'Just left the offices of Zynthe Gaming. Discussed new strategy. Zynthe will b hottest gaming co. in valley.' Did he not?"

Burke: "That's true. Maddox did consult with us but he received no compensation for his services."

Moderator: "And why was that?"

Burke: "Because we didn't consider his advice worth anything. Zynthe Gaming has never cut a check to Henry Maddox. Our auditors can attest to this fact."

"That was neatly done," Henry said.

"Henry, they're lying their butts off about you," Cheryl said.

"Yeah, but they're doing it well. There's an art to generating the lie most likely to be believed."

Moderator: "So from your perspective, Henry Maddox saw your success from a distance and viewed Laroy Elden's campaign as a way to get a piece of it."

Burke: "This is certainly not unusual when companies grow and prosper, especially to the degree Zynthe has. All sorts of people tend to come out of the woodwork. They all claim that the successful concept was their idea and they should in some way receive compensation. The desperate and immoral go so far as to extort you."

Moderator: "So Henry Maddox is a desperate, immoral extortionist?"

Burke: "Listen, I don't like talking about Henry Maddox this way. But I have to respond to the allegations against me and my company. I take my role of Chief Executive of Zynthe very seriously. There are many honest investors and employees who have given their lives to Zynthe. These people count on me to defend this type of garbage."

Moderator: "And so what should we make of the claims that he will disclose the destructive dealings of his other clients?"

Burke: "It's a bluff. And if he does make false allegations towards other companies, they will sue him for libel."

Moderator: "Will you sue Henry Maddox?"

Burke: "Frankly, I just want to move on and run a great business. I think all of this is going to blow over within a couple of days. I don't want to keep Maddox's name in the spotlight any longer than I have to."

Moderator: "Gerald Burke, thank you for your time."

Burke: "Thank you for having me."

"Well, that was disgusting," Cheryl said.

"No, Gerald actually performed really well," Henry said. "He came off as generous and above the fray. He marginalized Laroy and made me look petty. This interview will be replayed on every media outlet imaginable. By morning the story will no longer be about Zynthe, it will be about Laroy's and my character. And then the story will disappear entirely."

"So is that it? Game over?"

"Oh, I didn't say that," Henry said. "We still have a couple of tricks up our sleeve."

"Like what?" Pressley asked.

"Don't forget. We still have all of their data."

And there shall be many
 which shall say . . .
yea, lie a little,
take advantage of one
because of his words,
dig a pit for thy neighbor;
there is no harm in this;
and do all these things,
 for tomorrow we die . . .

- 2 Nephi 28:8, "The Book of Mormon"

CHAPTER 27

Four days after Henry posted his letter on henrymaddox.com, traffic to the site crested at over 30 million hits. A week later, visits had stabilized to about 10 million people each day. Most visits were brief. They were merely checking in to see if Henry had posted the list of companies referenced in his letter. Twitter followers had now grown from 5 million to 15 million. Henry was now within the top 10 most followed people on Twitter.

Though some of Henry's followers were detractors who wanted to monitor his posts, the majority had become supporters of the Destruction Is Not Profit campaign.

Laroy's cause had given focus, motivation, and voice to legions of people. These followers wanted Henry to be right.

Henry's letter and Burke's attack had created a national media firestorm. The public questions lingered. Was Henry the conniver who concocted a ploy to extort Zynthe? Or was he the convert for whom Laroy and his followers yearned?

Henry let the suspense build. Then, on a Tuesday morning He struck. Henry figured that if he could coax Burke into a fight on a Tuesday, he could steal the news cycle for the rest of the week.

> The list is up. C my clients and descriptions of the destructive strategies that each of these cos have used. henrymaddox.com.
> #destructionisnotprofit.

The landing page of henrymaddox.com showed a list of over one hundred businesses with descriptions of how each company profited at their consumer's personal (not just financial) expense. Most brands were well known, while some were smaller though well-funded startup companies.

Henry began by detailing the different sources of revenues for each of his clients. He highlighted the "partner revenue" item on each company's income statement and showed the true sources of those sales. Most of this money was derived from direct or indirect involvement in pornography, gambling, alcohol, and other vices. These disclosures gave support to Laroy Elden's latest "Destruction Is Not Profit" campaign, which focused on undisclosed, unsavory profit centers.

Henry's further revelations showed how his media clients worked hand-in-hand with their parent companies and subsidiary brands to break apart families through market fragmentation and propaganda campaigns. Henry used his largest client, Entz Media, as an example, breaking out Entz's strategies in exhaustive detail. Henry disclosed what he termed a "demographics ladder" that he used with Entz. The ladder showed a listing of different lifestyles, which were prioritized based on market potential and profitability. Henry showed how the more desirable demographics were the least commitment oriented. The most highly valued demographic was the single adult with no children. Henry cited specific examples of Entz Media campaigns that used film, television, and music to glamorize the single lifestyle and discourage marriage. Men were encouraged to be brutish, to use women to satisfy their carnal appetites. They partied and engaged in high-risk behaviors. Men were to seek pleasure at all costs.

Entz Media appealed to women in a more nuanced way. Women were encouraged to wait for an idealized, perfect man (who could never exist) before making commitments. They were taught to buy expensive clothing and accessories so their appearance would attract Prince Charming when he did appear. Women were encouraged to be promiscuous by pushing the notion that only sexual chemistry could reveal the perfect man.

Gender confusion was also a popular Entz strategy. If people were confused as to the correct gender of their perfect mate, it would further delay commitment. Entz

Media used their programming to glamorize alternative lifestyles and encourage sexual experimentation.

Within married households, the demographics ladder showed that dual incomes were preferred over single income households. Homes with no children were preferred above those with children. Unmarried partners with children were prioritized above committed, married couples with children.

Highlighted near the bottom of the demographic hierarchy was the traditional family with the comment, "no discretionary income" as a notation. That didn't mean that the traditional family went unnoticed, however. Henry showed how families without discretionary income were granted credit to consume beyond their needs. He noted that indebted families had a higher rate of divorce, which contributed to other needs and thus influenced other market opportunities.

Henry revealed the strategies Entz Media used to break marriages apart. Entz programming pushed the idea of marriage as being stale and uneventful and then glamorized a freer and more exciting life outside of marriage. Institutions that upheld chastity before marriage and fidelity within marriage were ridiculed. Storylines relating to religion centered on religious conspiracies and how people gained enlightenment apart from God, not from Him. The idea of commitment – to a wife, a child, a religion – was ridiculed. Selfishness was championed.

Entz Media went after children as well. The sexualized and gender confused teen ranked highly on the demographics ladder. So did the impressionable tween.

Television shows used exaggerated character types to encourage children and teenagers to label one another. Shows featured skaters, goths, gays, jocks, nerds, etc. Children and teenagers were encouraged to identify with one of the labels. Once an identity was embraced, corporations would then define the group's attributes and charge for compliance. Kid's programming was calculated to make them consume. Entertainment was no longer about story telling; it was story selling – social engineering.

Entz Media not only used financial metrics to track the success of their campaigns, they also tracked each campaign's influence on culture. Profitability was the short term measure of success. Cultural fragmentation was the pipeline to future opportunities. Henry shared the scorecard that he reviewed with Entz Media during his quarterly meetings. The charts were categorized by ethnicity, region, and income level. The trends were tracked over time. The data showed declining religious observance, declining marital rates, declining children born to married younger women, an increase in children born out of wedlock, etc. The statistics were convincing evidence that the cultural fragmentation strategies worked. Graphs showed how Entz's success in fragmenting markets was directly linked to increases in advertising, subsidiary, and parent corporation revenues.

Henry went on to show how recent data collection techniques have enhanced the fragmentation, formation, and targeting of the more desirable consumer groups. Data mining had grown to a $10 billion industry. Data miners had access to more than five thousand data elements on each person to place them into different micro target groups called "lifestyle clusters". Every purchase was tracked, every computer click was logged, even friend and neighbor's habits were monitored and analyzed; all with the motive of exploiting the target consumer for more profit.

Henry's revelations generated the buzz he was looking for. Supporters of henrymaddox.com lit up the chat forums with ideas on how to organize grassroots boycotts.

The mainstream media responded with . . . dead silence.

Not one major news organization even acknowledged the story. Gerald Burke issued one tweet on Wednesday, an entire day after Maddox's post.

Henry Maddox's rant = Laroy Elden's outdated traditions + Henry Maddox's hack theories. Desperation (sigh). #Timeforthisstorytogoaway

Henry, Pressley, and Cheryl were having lunch at a sandwich shop near Henry's office. No one spoke through the meal. Once finished, Pressley broke the silence. "I don't get it. You've handed over a smoking gun. Where's the public outrage?"

It was Thursday. The lack of response by Henry's clients had killed the momentum he had hoped to build. Even the blogs and chat rooms had now gone silent. He had to admit, it was well played.

"The corporations control the propaganda machines, Pressley," Henry said. "We can't force news organizations to cover what we think is important. Ultimately, media conglomerates will protect their corporate sponsors."

"What about our followers?" Cheryl asked. "They're organized and motivated. Why aren't they making more noise?"

"They're busy with their lives. This is the problem Laroy ran into for decades. People want excitement, not the truth. They want entertainment, not a call to action. Most people will only get involved if they feel that an imminent threat exists to them personally."

"Then what's the answer?" Cheryl asked.

Henry entered a tip amount and then signed the credit card receipt. He pushed the check into the middle of the table. "It's time to make this personal. Let's get to work."

Your right to swing your arms ends
just where the other man's nose begins.

- Zechariah Chafee (1919)

CHAPTER 28

The Following Week

Frank Salinger lived in an upper class neighborhood in South Lake, a suburb of Dallas. Frank was a practicing attorney, married, and had two children – twelve-year-old Justin and sixteen-year-old Courtney. He retrieved his mail that Wednesday evening and went back to the kitchen counter to sort through the collected items while his wife, Tricia finished making dinner.

Among the mailings was a 9 inch by 6 ¼ inch glossy postcard that said in bold, red, 48-point font:

Congratulations On Your Daughter
Courtney's Pregnancy!

The back of the card read:

Present This Card To Your Local Destination
Superstore
To Redeem Your Free Gift.

Pictures of different pregnancy and baby products with their associated prices surrounded the text of the postcard.

"People Are Not Products - henrymaddox.com" was written in 10-point font at the bottom of the postcard.

"Tricia, what is this?" Frank slid the postcard across the cold granite countertop to his wife.

"Courtney!" Tricia yelled. "Can you please come here for a minute?"

Courtney bounded down the stairs. "What's going on?"

Courtney's mom handed the postcard to Courtney. "Honey, do you know anything about this?"

Courtney's eyes welled up with tears. She then collapsed into her mother's arms.

———

Travis Baker lived in the middle class Bellevue, Washington, a suburb of Seattle. He was twenty two years-old and a recent college graduate in electrical engineering. He had also been unemployed for the past six months. Travis descended the stairs from his apartment, unlocked his mailbox, collected his mail, and quickly thumbed through the contents in hopes of receiving formal responses from some of his recent job interviews.

A 9 inch by 6 ¼ inch glossy postcard caught Travis' eye. In bold, red, 48-point font the postcard read:

Did You Know A Correlation Exists
Between People Who Listen To Rap Music,
Drive Compact Cars,
And Read Comic Books,
And Employees
Who Are Habitually Late To Work?

The back of the card then read:

Our Data Suggests
You Would Not Be A Good Fit For
Regional Semiconductor Co.
Thank You For Your Interest.

"People Are Not Products - henrymaddox.com" was written in 10-point font at the bottom of the postcard.

———

P am and Jim Cooper were renting a home in Alpharetta, Georgia when they retrieved a 9 inch by 6 ¼ inch glossy postcard from their mailbox. In bold, red, 48-point font the postcard read:

Thank You For Applying
For A Mortgage With Regional Bank.
You Have Impeccable Credit,

An Outstanding Debt To Income Ratio,
And The Home You Want To Purchase
Is Well Within Your Price Range.

The back of the card then read:

The Aggregate Data
Of Your Neighbors Suggests
People With Whom You Associate
Are Not Good Credit Risks.
Regional Bank Therefore Declines
Your Mortgage Application.

"People Are Not Products - henrymaddox.com" was written in 10-point font at the bottom of the postcard.

———

Helen Martinez went to her mailbox in the Los Angeles suburb of Palmdale, California to find a 9 inch by 6 ¼ inch glossy postcard. In bold, red, 48-point font the postcard read:

Helen,
Based On Your Internet Searches,
Grocery Store Purchases,
And Restaurant Receipts;
Our Data Suggests
You Are At Risk For Diabetes,
High Blood Pressure,

High Cholesterol,
And Heart Disease.

The back of the card then read:

Healthy Choice Health Insurers
Declines Your Health Insurance Renewal.

"People Are Not Products - henrymaddox.com" was written in 10-point font at the bottom of the postcard.

––––––

Charlotte Harmon was a Junior at a prestigious university in Boston Massachusetts when she received a 9 inch by 6 ¼ inch glossy postcard. In bold, red, 48-point font the postcard read:

Charlotte,
Your Academic Achievements
Have Preapproved You
For A Low Interest Rate Credit Card
From Priority Capital Credit.

In 18-point font, the back of the card then read:

Our Data Suggests That Within A Year,
You Will Become Employed
And Earn A Good Salary;

But Because You Are A Minority
And Your Parents
Are Not Highly Educated,
You Are Not Likely
Financially Sophisticated Enough
To Understand Our Credit Agreement.
We Therefore Feel We Can Entice You
To Accumulate Debt,
Trap You
Into A Perpetually High Interest Rate,
And Keep You In Poverty.
We Look Forward
To Profiting Handsomely
Off Of Our Relationship.

"People Are Not Products - henrymaddox.com" was written in 10-point font at the bottom of the postcard.

———

Laroy, Margaret, Pressley, Cheryl, and Henry all sat around the conference room table in Henry's office. The space was cramped and ill-suited for the types of war room discussions that had been held there over the past two weeks. The conference room projector cast the images generated by Cheryl's laptop as she clicked through different internet links. Each link displayed different, local media coverage of the People Are Not Products campaign.

"News organizations in over fifty different local markets have carried our story thus far," Cheryl said. "The different postcard scenarios you published have enraged people across the country. People are picketing, boycotting, and most importantly for us, registering on henrymaddox.com in record numbers. Our little army is growing."

"How many postcards did you send out in total Henry?" Margaret asked.

"About five thousand–"

"You leveraged a five thousand piece direct mail campaign into this sort of publicity?" Laroy asked. "You do know how to manipulate media, Henry."

"But didn't the media want to silence us?" Pressley asked.

"They still do," Henry said. "But to use a military term, we outflanked them."

"Outflank?"

"The big corporations are taking a top down approach to silence us. They've instructed their corporate heads to ignore our story entirely. Our direct mail campaign, however, went around the corporate heads directly into the local markets. The corporate heads don't want to publicize their hostility towards us too broadly for fear of blowback. So local affiliate stations don't realize how a local story like this will negatively affect the corporate interests of their parent companies.

"We sent a hundred or so postcards into every regional media market in the country, to people up and down the economic ladder. We identified fifty different scenarios that were assured to get the attention of each postcard recipient. Each local news organization had no choice but to cover the story. The fact that every local station covered the story forced the national news to at least comment on the mailings. We've exerted pressure from the bottom up . . . something the corporations can't control."

"Aren't you afraid the businesses that were named in the mailings will sue?" Pressley asked.

"Anyone can sue anyone for anything," Henry said. "In fact, we'll probably see a flurry of legal complaints within the next couple of days. This will give the businesses at least the perception that they are defending themselves against what they'll claim are false accusations. But we can afford attorney's fees. Each mailing we sent out gave voice to each business' true intention. I know because I orchestrated these same campaigns previously – albeit with much more subtlety. As Dostoevsky put it, '. . . intelligence is tortuous and sneaky. Intelligence is crooked, while stupidity is honest.' From a corporate perspective I did the stupidest thing that I could have done. I revealed the truth."

"Tell me this though Henry," Margaret said, "in one of your scenarios you identified teenage girls who were pregnant. How could you possibly know when many of the girls' parents didn't even know yet?"

"It's there in the data, though it took a little work to get it out. Historically, retailers would only know a woman was pregnant when she actually gave birth and the birth record was publicly available. These retailers would then flood the new mother with promotions to shop at their store. If a retailer could find out a woman was pregnant in the second trimester, rather than when the baby was born, that would give that store a tremendous advantage over their competition – once consumers establish purchasing habits, these behaviors aren't easily broken. This means the store that captures the new mother's business will enjoy a highly profitable revenue stream off of baby products for at least a couple of years.

"So there's an incentive for companies to accurately predict a woman's pregnancy as early as possible. Enter the geeks.

"Corporations now employ PHDs in Math, Statistics, Computer Science and other quantitative fields to scour millions of bits of data on each consumer. These analysts build computer models to detect variables that can be used to predict patterns. We call this practice 'predictive analytics.'"

"But what variables show that a woman is pregnant?" Pressley asked.

"You'd be surprised. The analysts identified hundreds of thousands of women who gave birth and then worked backwards to see what tendencies they developed during their pregnancies. A number of patterns emerged that when taken on their own didn't mean much – a change from buying scented to unscented lotion within the same month, or buying certain vitamin supplements. When you put these patterns together, the computer model began to predict pregnancies at the start of the second trimester almost without fail."

"And you had access to these computer models?" Margaret asked.

"I have data sharing agreements with all of my clients – well I guess former clients, now – that allow me access to these computer models."

"And so what you're telling me is that these analysts can build computer models that know more about us than our closest friends?" Margaret asked. "They've identified behaviors, life events, and habits that may have not even occurred yet?"

"And they can use this knowledge to get you to do or be what they want you to be," Henry said. "Combine this with the demographic ladder disclosure, and you can begin to see both the incentives and the means corporations have to produce fewer families and more dysfunction within society. It certainly doesn't bode well for the future of our communities."

"And now the student has become the teacher," Laroy said. "I must admit, I never would have imagined things would have become this sophisticated. I certainly couldn't have taken the cause to this level."

"Oh, Laroy," Henry said. "We're just getting started."

Nobody loves me,
but my mother,
And she could be jiving too.

- B.B. King

CHAPTER **29**

Gerald Burke opened the conference call with a collegial "good morning ladies and gents." He wanted to keep the conversation light and controlled.

Gerald was getting a lot of satisfaction out of the fraternity he'd established with Maddox's former clients. He was proving that, although just the captain of a startup, he could sit at the same table with the big boys.

"Henry Maddox has escalated the conflict," he said to his speaker phone. "In large part, we were successful in silencing his website disclosures about our business dealings. He's now countered with what he's called his 'People Are Not Products' campaign, where he exposes the way we use the data we've collected on our consumers. Knowing Henry, I suspect he still has a couple of tricks up his sleeve. I wanted to get everyone on a call to discuss a coordinated response."

"I haven't got to where I am in business by making decisions by committee Gerald," said a voice tinged with a southern accent – by tacit agreement, no one was using names. "We've tried a coordinated response and Maddox ran an end run around us. If I'm going to be responsible for the fallout of Henry Maddox's campaigns, I'm going to take control of my own response. I recommend each of you do the same. It's one thing for Maddox to fight a war on one front, but can he fight each of us independently?"

A measured northeastern accent then filled the air. "I'm with the last caller. We all know what tactics are at our disposal. I encourage each business interest on this call to use these tactics at your own discretion. We can overwhelm Maddox much more effectively by attacking him at the same time but yet independent of each other."

The unmistakable British Accent of Melvin Entz then sounded from Gerald's speaker. "Let's be honest here folks, Maddox has betrayed each of us personally. This man has been in my home, met my family, and dined at my table, and now he's in the process of destroying my business. I haven't spent my entire life building my media empire to see it taken down by some tosser who's suddenly found enlightenment, and I don't need Gerald Burke's permission to take off my gloves. To each his own on this one."

Melvin Entz's comments were punctuated by a click. Gerald could then here other participants dropping off of the call. So much for sitting at the table with the big boys.

Gerald lingered on the line. "Hello, is anyone still on the call?"

Gerald had lost his united front.

———

Henry left his Berkeley office around 7 pm. It was Friday night and he had asked Cheryl to meet him for dinner. He couldn't remember ever having a night time meal with Cheryl that didn't consist of take-out food at the conference table while they were putting out some fire or another. Henry asked Cheryl to dinner with the pretense of showing long-overdue appreciation for her years of loyalty at the firm. He hadn't touched on the real reason though. Cheryl was the only person in the world with whom Henry could confide. He needed to share how he felt with her, before it was too late.

They'd chosen a small restaurant in Walnut Creek named La Dolce. It was family run and had been in business for over twenty years. Henry's tastes normally ran more toward Kobe beef, white asparagus, and vintage brandy on exclusive rooftop restaurants. But tonight was about Cheryl, and if she wanted pasta and seafood in an informal setting, then so be it. Besides, the indulgence was losing its appeal.

Henry turned his Mercedes G550 and programmed his destination into the OnBoard GPS system. He needed to hurry if he was going to make their eight o'clock reservation.

Within minutes, Henry was swerving through traffic on State Route 24 approaching the Caldecott Tunnel. He slowed to merge as the traffic narrowed to two lanes. The only sound Henry could hear was the faint hum of the road beneath his tires. He used to avoid the quiet and would have had something on the sound system. Now he cherished the time for soul searching. He still had a long ways to go, but he could at last abide his own company, a reward that had taken an entire lifetime –

"Henry, do you really think you can get away with betraying your clients?"

Henry almost swerved off the road, then pivoted in his chair looking for the source of the voice. The back seats were empty.

"You're smart enough to know you can't run. And you certainly can't hide."

What? The voice was coming through the car's speaker system. Henry turned off the stereo.

The system turned itself back on. "Approaching the Caldecott Tunnel, Henry? You better hang on tight."

Henry reached for the radio again. But suddenly all four door locks snapped down with a click. He had a split second to recognize that he was in serious trouble when the car surged forward. Henry slammed on the brakes, but they made no difference.

"What?" the voice said. "You didn't know the OnBoard system could do that? If we can remotely unlock your doors, we can certainly lock you in the vehicle. If we can diagnose engine problems remotely, we can certainly tap into your car's computer system. OnBoard doesn't need your permission to mess with your fuel injection ratios, Henry. Did you really think collecting your data was the most threatening thing we could do?"

Henry kept his hands on the wheel, trying to breathe evenly. He crossed the threshold into the tunnel, where he now only had two lanes and no shoulders. He darted around a slower car in front of him, then leaned on the car's horn and began flashing his lights to warn the other drivers.

"Oh there you go Henry, I guess the horn still works, eh?"

The blind panic was beginning to fade, and his mind was kicking into high gear. Whoever this was, they were willing to kill him and didn't care if they took other people with him.

Talk. He needed to talk. It was what he did best.

"So you're going to kill me and make it look like an accident?" Henry asked. "I expected as much, but I thought you'd have more decency than to take others with me. Or is that collateral damage?"

"You're destroying billions of dollars of wealth creation, Henry. Certainly people have been killed for much less. Even innocent ones."

The emergency brake! Henry yanked up on the cable, only to see the RPMs climb on his dash console. He could feel the drag of the brake, but his speed persisted. He tried to jam the gearshift into neutral but the gear stayed frozen in drive.

Henry swerved to avoid another car. The Mercedes was now going ninety miles per hour through traffic flowing at seventy. He snapped the ignition off. No effect.

Up ahead were brake lights in both lanes.

He had to make a call. Henry swerved from left to right in one quick, sudden motion, angling into the inner wall of the tunnel. Sparks flew as he kept the steering wheel turned to the far right. The passenger airbag deployed.

He was only about one hundred yards from the vehicle in front of him and still closing.

Henry straightened the car, then drove it back into the tunnel wall. This time, he increased the angle.

His tires grabbed the asphalt and launched the car into the air. Glass shattered and the driver's side airbag deployed, knocking Henry back into his seat. The car slid down the highway, driver's side down. Henry's left arm burned as the friction heated the driver's door. He contorted his body away from the pavement sliding less than a foot from his face.

Blood dripped into his eyes, making it hard to see. Pieces of glass from the windshield peppered his face.

The sliding car came to a rest. He heard the screeching from other drivers behind him and braced for impact.

It never came. No other cars crashed. No one else would get hurt.

He felt his mental grasp slipping.

"Cheryl," he whispered.

Then things went black.

Life is painting a picture,
not doing a sum.

- Oliver Wendell Holmes, Jr.

CHAPTER 30

"Mr. Entz, welcome to Washington D.C. Things are pretty quiet here on Saturdays, but given the urgency of your request I've reached out to some influential people who have agreed to meet with you."

"I should hope so," Entz said. "My Political Action Committee has spread millions of dollars around this town."

Jack Buston, former Congressman from New York and the most powerful lobbyist in DC, led Melvin Entz to an awaiting town car. Jack opened the door for Entz before removing his black fedora and folding his large frame into the back seat beside him. Within minutes, the town car was gliding from the private airstrip to Jack's office on K Street. Melvin Entz had never practiced small talk. It was widely known that he viewed banter as weakness. Each statement was calculated to achieve a purpose. So Jack chose his words carefully.

"Mr. Entz, I've assembled a team of people at my office. Though you'll not see any elected representatives, many of their legislative aides and chiefs of staff will be in the room.

I hope you understand that elected officials like to keep these types of discussions at arm's length."

"All I care about are results Jack. I gave money to these pillocks' campaigns. I got them elected. Today I'm here for payback."

"I understand sir. Within the room will be representation from members of both the House and the Senate. I've chosen to invite those that have influence on the Committee on Homeland Security and Government Affairs, the Select Committee on Intelligence, and the Committee on Commerce, Science, and Transportation. Specifically I think the subcommittees on Commerce, Manufacturing, and Trade as well as Communications, Technology, and the Internet will be of particular use for us. I've also invited people connected to the Federal Trade Commission, because a breach of user privacy may be a useable angle for us."

"Do those in the room have an understanding of my problem?"

"I've already had preliminary discussions with most of them. Our feeling is that we can force Maddox to turn over all his data in the interest of national security. We can impose a Cease and Desist order on his operations based on user privacy and trade infractions. We can even drag him before congress if you like."

"No. I don't want to give any more publicity to this scoundrel."

"I understand. Our objective will be to shut him down quietly, using the full force of the government's resources."

"It's time Maddox learns who really controls this great country of ours," Entz said. "It's a shame it had to come to this. He had such a promising mind."

———

"Henry can you hear me? Nurse, he looks like he's opening his eyes."

Cheryl?

"Mr. Maddox, stay still," another voice said. "You're in the hospital. You've had quite a shock to your system. Try to take things slowly."

Henry tried to move his hands but they were tied to the bed railings. "My arms . . ."

"We didn't want you to pull off your monitors."

Consciousness was slowly flowing back. Cheryl, looking relieved to the point of tears, was standing behind a woman in a brightly-colored polyester jumper. Her name tag read . . . he realized he still couldn't make it out. "Monitors?"

"Yes, we're monitoring your heartbeat, your oxygen level, and your blood pressure. We also have you on an IV."

"How long?"

"You arrived around nine o'clock last night by ambulance. You were in quite a car accident."

Taneesha. The nurse's name was Taneesha. "Anyone else hurt?"

"No, you were the only one."

"Henry, it's me." Cheryl pushed past Taneesha and grabbed his hand.

He managed a smile. "Sorry I didn't make dinner."

"Don't worry Henry, I had a craving for hospital cafeteria food anyway."

Cheryl's warm smile relaxed Henry.

"How long . . . you been here?"

"I got here around ten o'clock last night. The hospital called me. Did you know I'm listed as your only emergency contact through the DMV?"

"Sounds right." A smirk crossed Henry's lips. "Am I okay?"

"You're in remarkably good shape for what you've been through Mr. Maddox," Taneesha said. "You suffered an acute subdural hematoma that caused you to lose consciousness. Can you move your toes for me Mr. Maddox?"

Henry wiggled his toes.

"And now please lift up your left arm and then your right arm."

They felt unexpectedly heavy, but Henry complied.

"Does that mean no risk of paralysis exists?" Cheryl asked.

"It's certainly a good sign," the nurse said. "When he feels up to it, we'll let him walk around the hospital. We also need to do some tests to assure his mental faculties are okay. I'll leave you two alone. It will be good for him to talk."

Taneesha grabbed a clipboard and exited the room.

"Do you remember what happened last night Henry?"

It came back to him. The car taken over, out of control. "Yes."

Henry began to drift off to sleep again.

"Henry," Cheryl's stern inflection startled Henry back to consciousness. "Tell me about the accident."

"They took over my car Cheryl."

Cheryl ran her fingers through his hair. "Who's they, Henry?"

"The OnBoard people. Or someone who hacked into OnBoard. I don't know. It doesn't really matter, anyway."

"Of course it matters. We need to report whoever did this to the police."

"Couldn't prove it. Forensics would only show . . . car's computer system screwed up."

"But you can tell them what happened."

He laughed a laugh that was half cough. "I can see the headlines. 'Henry Maddox claims GPS system high jacked his car.' That's exactly what they want me to say. Ruin my credibility for good."

"But we can't let them get away with this."

"People are nasty. Too much money at stake for too many. They want my credibility or my life, one or the other."

"Then let them win Henry." Cheryl stroked Henry's cheek with the back of her fingers. "Save your life. There's no shame in that. You've made your point."

"I need to undo what I've done–"

"Even if that means your life?"

"Anything less wouldn't be . . ." losing his struggle, Henry faded back to sleep.

No man is clever enough
to know all the evil he does.

- François de la Rochefoucauld

CHAPTER 31

Four Days Later

Maddox approached the door of his Berkeley office, fighting a light-headedness that was either from the concussion or the pain meds. He fumbled for the doorknob and let the weight of his body push the door open.

"Henry!" Cheryl said. "You need to get back into bed, and now. The doctor said you needed to take at least a couple more days before resuming work."

"I know, but we can't waste the momentum we've created. We need the next campaign out this week. If we blow the timing, they've won."

"Can't you let me help Dr. Maddox?" Pressley asked.

"Thanks, but I need to insulate each of you from these campaigns. You need to be able to deny knowledge of what's about to occur."

"You're not thinking about doing anything crazy are you?" Cheryl asked.

"That ship sailed a while ago. I just need to do a couple of things from the office and then I can do the rest from home."

Henry retreated to his office and fired up his computer. A couple of clicks later, and he was relieved to find hackers hadn't cut him off from his data. The extra money he'd spent insulating the server farm was paying off. He started some data analytics and initiated some batch transfers.

An hour later, Henry heard Cheryl's voice in reception. Then, a minute later, "Henry, some gentlemen are here to see you."

Henry went out to her desk to find two men with dark suits talking to Cheryl. "How can I help you gentlemen?"

"Hello Dr. Maddox, my name is Agent Terry and this is Agent Parker, we're with the Department of Homeland Security."

"I see. Cheryl, would you mind taping this, please?"

She gave a sweet smile. "I've already turned on the cameras."

The agents glanced at one another but maintained their poker faces. "As you're aware," Parker said, "we have the right to examine the type of data you're collecting on citizens of this country."

"That shouldn't be a problem. I'm not collecting any data. I've merely licensed data from numerous other primary sources. If you have a problem with the type of data in my possession, your problem is really with these primary sources, not with me. I can have Cheryl show you the relevant agreements we have with each source."

"The concern extends further than the data itself, Dr. Maddox. You should know that the Federal Trade Commission has received complaints from citizens objecting to the way you are using the information."

"Again, if the Federal Trade Commission has a problem with the way I'm using people's data, they really have a problem with the primary source, not with me. I'm not doing anything these primary sources haven't done before. To indict me is to indict my sources. To indict my sources will actually be a tremendous benefit to me and my campaigns. I will happily comply with whatever investigation you feel–"

"I don't think you understand," Agent Parker said. "We aren't here to investigate. We're here to shut you down."

Both agents produced gold, reflective badges with bold lettering encircling an insignia of an eagle spreading its wings.

"Ah. Perhaps you're not as aware of my legal rights as I am." Henry said. "Section 9 of the FTC Act authorizes the Commission to 'require by subpoena the attendance and testimony of witnesses and the production of all such documentary evidence related to any matter under investigation.' Once I receive the subpoena, under Commission Rule 2.7, I have the right to object by filing a petition to limit or quash. My petition would then be referred to a designated Commissioner and the designated Commissioner's ruling could be appealed to the full Commission. Of course subsequent to the FTC Improvements Act of 1980, the Bureau of Consumer

Protections may now use what they call 'civil investigative demands' or CIDs but the process is essentially the same as a subpoena.'

The expressionless agents looked at each other again before directing their attention back to Henry.

"Now if you violate my due process, you would be disciplined and any case against me would, of course, be compromised. So before you start rifling through all of my files in some sort of fishing expedition, I thought I might advise you as to my understanding of the law. So how would you like to proceed?"

Agent Terry looked at Agent Parker. Agent Parker shook his head.

"Thank you for your time Dr. Maddox," Agent Terry said.

"Very well, gentlemen. Have a good day."

As Agent Terry and Agent Parker marched out of the office, Pressley began to clap quietly.

"That was awesome, Dr. Maddox," she said. "You put them in their place."

"Only for the moment," Henry said. "They're exploring different angles. We're well within our legal rights to do what we've done, but that doesn't mean they can't turn our office inside out and make life difficult for us. We've only bought some time. Let's put it to use."

———

Henry sequestered himself in his San Francisco home for the remainder of the week. He spoke to no one. He spent his time with the data. The People Are Not Products campaign showed how predictive analytics models had transformed the traditional business-to-consumer relationship. In a sudden bizarre twist, people now realized they were not only the customers of a given business, they were also the product. Companies tracked each customer's every move and profited from the information. None of them worried that this evolution compromised privacy and challenged civil liberties. Henry had now pointed that out rather dramatically.

But it wasn't enough. Predictive analytics extended far beyond the business to consumer relationship. The logic of predictive analytics was now embedded into the heart of the world's financial system.

Wall Street Banks and hedge funds employed the most brilliant analytical minds in the world – 'quants,' as they were called, with PHDs in math, computer science, and economics, and sometimes all three. They built computer programs geared to analyze market patterns, reverse engineering trading behavior to capture correlations between groupings of variables and trades. When the right cocktail of variables satisfied a given algorithm, the computer triggered an exchange that beat the predicted, legitimate trade within a nanosecond. High-frequency traders booked billions of dollars every year off of these kinds of trades – at the expense of real investors. Markets that were originally formed to provide capital to promising companies and a return to informed investors were now being gamed by manipulators. The quants and the people who hired them made money, but they risked bringing down the entire system.

And that wasn't the worst of it. Computer models now formed the basis for a significant number of the trades on financial markets. Thousands of algorithms interfaced with each other in what now amounted to a large black box of logic that no one thoroughly understood. When these algorithms worked as intended, traders made loads of money. But no machine always worked as intended.

At 2:45 p.m. EDT on May 6, 2010, the DOW Jones Industrial Average lost 1,000 points in twenty minutes.

After a five-month investigation, the SEC and the CFTC concluded that the "flash crash," as it was known, revealed the fragility and sophistication of the current markets. Congressional hearings also examined the event. But lobbyists for the financial markets challenged the conclusions of both studies, offering their own expert opinions, and in the end nothing was done. And the markets were as vulnerable now as they were then.

Henry cracked his knuckles above his keyboard. It was time to remind people of that fact.

You say that this
wasn't in your plan
Don't mess around
with the demolition man

- The Police
"Demolition Man" (1981)

CHAPTER 32

The day began like any other. Traders on Wall Street clutched a 10-percent-recycled-paper cup of coffee in one hand and a designer, leather laptop satchel in the other as they made their way to their offices. Town cars and taxis formed processions in front of skyscrapers with company logos chiseled on the buildings' stone facades. The July Manhattan humidity caused these men and women to perspire, momentarily, during their brief jaunt from the street curb to the front doors of their buildings.

It was Monday and office conversations focused on soccer games in the suburbs and weekend outings to vacation homes in The Hamptons. No major economic news was expected for the day. Trading volume was assumed to be light. Anxiety over the European debt crisis still lingered, but the market had grown weary of reacting to the alternating austerity plans and bail-out solutions under constant consideration. The tension was still present, though, lingering in the algorithms like a ghost in the machine.

At 9:17, a series of buy orders, funded by a single offshore, Swiss account but funneled through various trading accounts, dumped 100 million dollars into credit default swaps insuring specific Euro Zone countries against sovereign debt defaults. The movement, indicating fear of Euro Zone collapse, triggered a number of other algorithms to increase the trading volume on these securities exponentially. By 9:19, 30 billion dollars had flowed into credit default swaps.

Lots of money chasing the same product had an easily predictable effect – the price of credit default swaps went up by ten percent, attracting the attention of the high-frequency traders. By 9:19:30, the securities were trading at much larger volume than they had seen in over a year.

The markets began to take notice. What did people know? Traders and investors alike scoured financial news sources. Cell phone rings interrupted government representatives throughout the world, as powerful financial minds sought to gain further insight into European markets. By 9:24, the yields on Greek, Irish, Portuguese, Spanish, and Italian bonds all began to climb.

At 9:26, the initial credit default swaps were liquidated – at a 400% profit. The half billion flowed into U.S. Treasuries and Japanese Yen – both traditional safe havens from exposure in Europe.

The 10 percent market rise and significant volume in European credit default swaps, combined with the simultaneous rise in U.S. Treasuries and Japanese Yen, triggered the electronic equivalent of panic in computer models.

By 9:31, while traders were still trying to understand the initial rise in credit default swaps, the Euro lost 30 percent in value as bank computers around the world began to dump the currency. All major indices began to crater.

By 9:34, banking stocks had dropped 25 percent. Businesses with heavy interests in Europe lost 20 percent. Gold and silver rose 10 and 12 percent respectively.

Detecting massive, sudden declines in many securities, computer algorithms from the six "market making firms" triggered circuit breakers that cut off all trading. Although engineered to safeguard these banks from irrational market behavior, in this instance the circuit breakers had an unanticipated effect. The algorithms froze liquidity. Exchanges began to dry up.

By 9:37, market information was growing obscure. Computer trading platforms hit lags of up to two seconds in trying to align buyers and sellers. Popular individual stocks became volatile. One widely held stock fell 20 percent in as many seconds. The precipitous fall brought down all indices.

Full-blown panic reigned.

The major exchanges began to interfere with the markets. They began to route trades to computer platforms under less strain. Floor traders jumped in at so called "liquidity replenishment points" to restore order. By 9:42, major indices were down 15 percent and falling.

At 9:43, the half-billion moved back out of U.S Treasuries and Japanese Yen at basis, which was now 10 percent below market.

This large, irrational trade – who would sell a position worth $550 million for a mere $500? – further confused the logic within the automated trading systems. Trades from some of the smaller firms accelerated while others shut down completely. The value of U.S. Treasuries and Japanese Yen now began to fall in concert with the Euro. Why were traders fleeing traditional safe havens? This was no longer about European solvency; this was now about the integrity of the entire financial system.

By 9:50, talk of cyber terrorism was spreading within financial circles. Stock exchanges throughout the world began shutting down. Less than an hour after the NYSE opening bell, all the world markets had ceased trading.

Henry closed his laptop with a smile. It really was remarkable what you could do if you understood the data.

———

World financial markets were still closed on Tuesday, when Henry issued the following press release on henrymaddox.com:

> When, in 1850, Frédéric Bastiat, coined the term "Destruction Is Not Profit" he could never have imagined the myriad of ways that successive generations would violate his principle.

During our campaigns, we have attempted to expose the ways that people profit to the detriment of their neighbors. Some of these campaigns have been more obvious than others. More recently, we have illustrated how massive data collection allows those that possess this information to predict *your* future and profit off of that knowledge. The "People Are Not Products" campaign has shown that no one is safe. We have made these issues personal and we got your attention.

Unbeknownst to many, the financial markets have used data collection to similar ends. Some of the smartest people within some of the most respected financial companies in the world have written computer programs that use data to predict trades. These computer algorithms are remarkably accurate. They allow traders to profit at the expense of legitimate investors.

Yesterday, however, we saw the damage that can occur when these computer programs are manipulated. Someone who understood the logic behind predictive analytics and computerized high frequency trading platforms crippled the entire world financial system.

That someone was me. My apologies to those who were hurt, but I needed to get your attention.

How long can we as a culture thrive when we step on others to get ahead? How long will we reward companies who manipulate and exploit over those who produce and innovate? We have allowed firms to transform the most sophisticated trading market in the history of the world into a high stakes casino. And then rig the game. And if you're not upset yet, wait until the government uses your tax dollars to make these traders whole for their recent losses. You see, unlike a casino, when these gamblers win, they win, when they lose, *you* lose.

This is not a problem of capitalism. In fact, this is not capitalism. Nor is this endemic to a republican democracy. This is a problem of each of us, as individuals. No system of government and no form of commerce can survive when corruption reigns. No network of computers can replace the enlightened human mind. Virtue must temper self interest. We must all become accountable and we must do it now.

I will issue a campaign tomorrow that can begin to reverse the manipulation. Consumers still have a voice. Will you use it?

*The young man
knows the rules,
but the old man
knows the exceptions.*

- Oliver Wendell Holmes, Jr.

CHAPTER 33

As soon as he saw Henry Maddox's press release, Melvin Entz was on the phone with Jack Buston.

"Jack, you were supposed to put this guy in a box! Why is he now taking credit for yesterday's flash crash?"

"It's complicated, Mr. Entz."

"No, it's not. I'm paying you and other public officials to look out for my interests. Henry Maddox is a threat to those interests, what more do I have to say?"

"We sent Federal agents over to Maddox's office. He doesn't scare easily, and any legal action we take against him will take time. The premise of any complaint could implicate your business practices as well. This is a very delicate issue—"

"The man just admitted to taking down the world financial system. How is that not a crime?"

"Maddox didn't act on any non-public information to make his trades. He just took advantage of the existing market anxiety."

"He's claiming he knew the logic of high-frequency trading algorithms of the biggest traders in the world. Isn't that proprietary information?"

"Technically, no. The logic of these algorithms were disclosed to him by his clients. He has agreements showing that. So there's no breach of security. Furthermore, traders who use *their* knowledge of the high frequency trading algorithms to profit can't be prosecuted. How can we prosecute Maddox for doing the same thing – only in reverse?"

"The man is a terrorist, Jack!"

"The man is brilliant, Mr. Entz. We can't find any legal way to shut him down without bringing down everyone he's fighting against. And believe me, we've spent night and day trying."

"Jack, I don't want to hear any more excuses. I want this man silenced before another one of his campaigns costs me money. Seeing how Maddox's next campaign is scheduled for tomorrow, you better get to work."

———

Gerald Burke sat across the desk from Zynthe's in-house Legal Counsel. "Do you mean to tell me that no legal angle exists to stop Henry Maddox?"

"What I'm telling you is that any angle we take against Maddox could be used against us as well. If we attack him for using our user's data in his campaigns, we'll implicate Zynthe in the same practice. If we challenge the data sharing agreement allowing him access to our user's data, we publicize to the world that such data sharing agreements exist. If users truly understood the extent of the data we collect and share with others, no one would play our games. Our only way to fight against him is to admit he's right."

"Sean, I have put too much into this company to see it fail. Maddox has attracted too much attention. He has credibility. People are listening to him."

"The question for you, Gerald, is how far are you willing to go to stop him?"

———

First Affinity Bank and Trust was one of the five largest banks in the world. As was the case with the other four banks, First Affinity was also one of the largest traders on Wall Street. Only First Affinity Chief Executive Lewis Chase knew the true extent of the bank's losses in the latest flash crash. The question now was, how to spin a 10.6 billion dollar loss to the public. The spectacle of such a loss could finally provide the resolve the government needed to restrict his bank's trading activity for good.

Instead of disclosure, Lewis Chase had one last card to play that might save him from disgrace . . . distraction. Lewis played this card on the top rated morning news program in the country.

"To each person that suffered a market loss yesterday, First Affinity Bank and Trust can feel your pain. Yesterday was the blackest day in the history of world financial markets. Unlike natural disasters that ravage our communities, this catastrophe had a cause and a culprit. The contagion that transmitted yesterday's virus had a name – Henry Maddox."

Lewis Chase's accusation set off a fire storm of discussion. Other Chief Executives of financial firms and publicly traded corporations followed his lead. When asked about the effect of black Monday's flash crash on their company's financials, they all pivoted the discussion to the same place. Blame Henry Maddox.

———

Henry saw his iPhone light up and vibrate. Cheryl again. He really wanted to talk to her but the time wasn't right, not yet.

Maddox sat across from a young man he strained to recognize. "Benjamin?"

"Yes, Mr. Maddox, it's me, Benjamin."

"Wow, you look like a new person."

"Yeah, I've completed my therapy here at New Beginnings and now I volunteer a couple of days a week. I like to help others here at the facility. I feel like I can relate to them. I try to give them hope in their future; something I thought I'd lost."

"I wanted to make sure you saw Benjamin while you were here." Jennifer Bennet's massive smile punctuated the sentence. "He's one of our greatest success stories. I'm pleased you found our organization worthy of your donation. It was kind of you to come by in person to deliver it. Proper funding will help us reach many more young people like Benjamin."

Henry reached into the pocket of his sport coat and pulled out an envelope.

"Please don't open this until I leave Jennifer. Oh, and I don't want this gift to be publicized. Maybe just keep it between us two?"

"Deal." Jennifer extended a firm handshake to Henry.

Energized from seeing Benjamin's progress and Jennifer's appreciation, Henry turned and left the facility. Just as he was at the door, he heard a jubilant shout.

He'd have given them more, but there was a point where too much money could undermine what they were trying to do. He settled on $25 million.

Henry got into his car and dialed Cheryl. He got her voicemail. "Cheryl, this is Henry. I got your message. I still need to talk to you, but the timing never seems to be right. I'll call you later. Stay safe. Henry."

Henry arrived at Laroy's house at 4 o'clock in the afternoon. Laroy met him at the door.

"Good to see you Henry. I'm glad you came by. I've been thinking about all of this data. Why don't we just destroy it and be done with it? Seeing the types of things *you* can do with the data, I'm coming to believe no one should be trusted with so much information, with so much power. The next, impressionable generations don't stand a chance. Media companies already have a propaganda pipeline into every home in this country via television and the internet. Now with all these new forms of media and tracking, even the best of parents won't be able to control the messaging their kids are fed. Corporate interests will coax young people into living purposeless and indulgent lives – all while they make mountains of money off of their 'key demographics.'"

"I think you're right, but as a practical matter, you can't destroy the data. Every person's data has been stored, replicated, and analyzed in so many different ways, erasing it all would be impossible."

"And this flash crash you caused yesterday? This is more than protecting children. This is about protecting our entire economic system, our political system . . . everything, everyone." Laroy paused. "Where are my manners? Let's talk about this inside."

"I wish I could. I don't have time."

"What is it?"

"I really just wanted to stop by and say goodbye."

"What? Where are you going?"

"They're closing in on me. And I'm starting to become the entire story. The only way for the cause to survive is for me to disappear."

"They . . . meaning your old clients?" Laroy's face was sober, concerned. "Henry, we can get you protection."

"No, you really can't. Protection wouldn't have prevented what happened in the Caldecott Tunnel. Someone somewhere will find a way to get to me. There are too many of them. There's too much at stake. They're running out of options."

"Where will you go? What will you do?"

"I'll think of something."

"How can I help you, Henry?"

"Keep the cause going. Look out for Pressley and Cheryl."

"I can't generate these campaigns like you can Henry. I won't be able to sustain the energy."

"You don't have to. Do you remember what you originally asked me to do? You wanted a voice. One that would be heard. I've given that to you. You now have a vast, attentive audience. What will you say when the whole world is listening?"

"But if the data is the problem, and it can't be destroyed, what good will my voice do?"

"Oh, I'm sorry, I forgot. I've got that covered."

"What? How?"

"Simple. We can't destroy the data, but we can corrupt it."

"I'm sorry, I don't understand the distinction."

"Stay tuned."

Close up his eyes
and draw the curtain close . . .

- Shakespeare, "King Henry VI"

CHAPTER 34

Henry spent the night in his Berkeley office. He parked his candy apple red, Audi R8 three blocks away behind a bakery. The aggressive lines, low profile, and expansive air intakes typically attracted the most unlikely of admirers. Even hippie street performers would stop and gape at the masterpiece. But tonight, with the moonless sky and inconspicuous location the vehicle went unnoticed. Henry had initially bought the car to turn heads, make an impression . . . to make a splash. All of which he intended to do first thing in the morning.

He kept the office lights off and lay on the floor, covering himself with a jacket. From the outside, the office appeared empty. Those looking for Henry drove by the office and not seeing any evidence of his presence, rerouted to his San Francisco home.

Henry knew they would be back, but probably not until morning. They would spend the night staking out his home. Once they learned he wasn't there either, they'd come to the office and interrogate Cheryl. He needed to be at the office to protect her. Tomorrow, he would end this standoff once and for all.

All of the details were set. Only the execution remained. It was for precisely this reason he couldn't rest. So Henry did what he should have done many hours before, he called Cheryl.

"Hi, sorry to call so late."

"I've been worried about you all day. Are you all right?"

"Oh, fine. Listen, tomorrow's going to be an eventful day and I want you to promise me something."

"What's that?"

"That you'll stay safe."

"What's going to happen?"

"I can't tell you the details, but I suspect that when you come to open the office in the morning, you'll have some company. They don't want you, they want me. Don't stand in their way. I have a plan. You have to trust me. Just don't do anything rash."

"Okay, so you just want me to open the office at 8 o'clock in the morning, as usual."

"That's all you need to do. And Cheryl, there's one more thing. I'd hoped to tell you in person, but tomorrow might get a little crazy."

"Yes."

Henry paused and took a deep breath.

"Of all the mistakes I've made in my life, there's one that stands out . . . one where I can't forgive myself."

"What's that?"

"I wish I could've lived a life worthy of you."

Thirty seconds of silence followed.

"Henry, I don't like these final terms? Maybe we still have a chance?"

"My very presence puts you in danger, Cheryl. The one thing worse than not being with you would be if I were to somehow lead to someone harming you."

"Why don't we go somewhere together? Just you and me?"

"We'd have to always be on the run. I could never ask that of you. I've made my bed. You still have a life in front of you. When I'm gone, they'll leave you alone."

"When you're gone?" Cheryl's voice cracked. "What does that mean?"

"Again, just know that I have a plan. That's all I can say. I'm sorry. It's for your own protection. I'll see you in the morning."

Henry hung up and lay down again. He wasn't comfortable, particularly. It wasn't as if he could sleep anyway. His mind was focused on his exit strategy.

He sat up and reached for his laptop. He had already written his henrymaddox.com campaign message. He thought he'd review it one more time before publishing it.

Henrymaddox.com believes in the capital markets. Capitalism has provided more goods and services, which satisfy more wants and needs, than any other system in history. Capitalism has rewarded the industrious, fed, clothed, and housed countless people, and led to untold innovations – without formal orchestration or compulsion. All thanks to Adam Smith's "invisible hand."

When self-interest triumphs over virtue, however, the entire system of capitalism is compromised and everyone loses! Henrymaddox.com envisions a world where economics work - for everyone. Our focus has thus been to educate consumers. The "Destruction Is Not Profit" campaigns have exposed shortsighted businesses that profit at the expense of others. We want the market to put these companies out of business. The "People Are Not Products" campaign illustrated how the collection of your most personal data allows computer models to predict your future moves. This evolution provides businesses with unprecedented powers of persuasion.

We want to turn the tables on those who collect and use our data in ways we never contemplated. You have the power to take your data back. You have the power to render the data meaningless.

DO YOUR PART: Over the next couple of weeks, we want you to change your consumption behaviors. Shop at different stores, buy different brands, and encourage complete strangers to use your loyalty cards. Shop with cash instead of credit cards. Don't play video games that seek to gather data about you or your friends. If you do, make stuff up. Visit websites that hold no interest for you. Click on as many pay-per-click banner ads as you can. Change your social network profiles to reveal as little as possible about you. Then admit all sorts of people to your social network – people with whom you would never associate.

You see, you can't destroy your data. But you can corrupt it. You can bury the good data in mountains of bad data. Your data will therefore become useless for marketers. Watch with satisfaction as you receive ads via direct mail and email that miss the target. Notice the banner ads on your web pages that have no correlation with your true interests.

Reverse the manipulation. Part of being an educated consumer is knowing what leverage you have and how to use it. Force businesses to be accountable.

"Destruction is not profit."
– Frederic Bastiat (1850)

"People are not products."
– Henry Maddox (2013)

It was now four o'clock in the morning Pacific Time. Maddox published the blog entry. He would steal the morning news cycle one more time. And then, a couple of hours later, he would create the story of the day. The new story would drive more traffic to henrymaddox.com than the site had ever known. It would be Henry's last great promotion.

Henry checked the upcoming day's San Francisco weather on his iPhone. At ten o'clock in the morning it looked to be sixty degrees and foggy, with winds from the west at forty five miles per hour across the Golden Gate Bridge. All looked according to plan.

The answer my friend
is blowin' in the wind.

- Bob Dylan (1962)

CHAPTER 35

The anticipation of the day had drained Henry's energy. That, combined with a sleepless night and his not yet full recovery from the Caldecott tunnel episode, made him worry that he might not be sharp enough to carry out his plan. All he needed was a couple of intense, focused hours and it would all be over.

The rattling of Cheryl's keys sent a much needed shot of adrenaline up Henry's spine, rejuvenating him.

Cheryl entered the office at exactly eight o'clock in the morning. She ran through the door and straight to Henry's office. She paused in the doorway, wiping her swollen, teary eyes.

Henry stood, staring at her. He would typically catch himself and avert his gaze. Not this time.

Cheryl's sudden advance broke Henry's concentration. She threw her arms around him, pulling him close to her. He held her in his arms. Neither Cheryl nor Henry could find words. Cheryl pulled back from Henry just far enough for him to kiss her trembling lips. Years of devotion left unsaid finally communicated.

Enveloped in Cheryl's arms, Henry's thoughts turned to an alternate fate. Maybe they could still be together?

A sudden crash of shattering glass broke Henry's concentration and jolted him back to the present.

"Cheryl, no," Henry said.

Despite his warning, Cheryl darted around the corner to see two, bulging thugs walking through the office's entrance. The force of the men kicking in the door had shattered the door's smoked glass pane.

"Haven't you ever heard of knocking?" Cheryl shouted.

A protruding vein pulsated from the first man's bald head as he advanced toward Cheryl. "We're here for Maddox. Where is he?" The first man asked.

Henry sauntered around the corner and paused long enough for the men to identify him.

"There he is, get him," the bald one shouted as he blitzed Henry like a wrecking ball.

Henry turned and ran for the back door. Both men pursued, but he had the lead. Once outside, Henry went towards the bakery. He needed at least sixty seconds of separation to get to his car. He was betting on the morning bakery rush.

Henry shoved his way through the crowd and hopped the counter, slipping as he landed. His head was spinning – effects from the accident. Not now, too much at stake. Henry stumbled to his feet and made it to the rear exit. In the wake of the excitement, customers pushed towards the cashier to see the source of commotion. The sudden surge by the bakery patrons blocked his assailants.

Yes! Trust people to behave predictably.

Henry piled into the Audi and pressed a button to start the engine – no fumbling for keys, nice. The two thugs appeared in his rear view mirror. The bald one made it to the car first and managed to grab the only thing that stuck out on the aerodynamic wonder – the windshield wiper. Henry snapped the car into gear, and the Audi took off like a rocket, leaving the wiper in the man's hand with the wiper arm now bent out of place but still attached to the car.

But Henry wasn't done with these two. He turned toward Center Street, then stopped and revved the engine.

Within seconds the two thugs jumped into a 2004 Pontiac GTO driven by a third, and headed in Henry's direction.

Although other avenues would have been faster, Henry needed fanfare. He wove in and out of traffic on Center Street, holding the Audi back just enough that the GTO stayed in line. Then, after a few blocks, two Town Car limousines and a familiar Porsche joined the procession. Gerald Burke, Melvin Entz, and Lewis Chase.

Well. He had himself a parade.

Once he arrived at University Avenue, more than eight vehicles were tracking him. Henry punched the accelerator as he approached the onramp for southbound Interstate 580. The nineteen inch aluminum wheels clenched the asphalt as the 5.2 liter, V10 engine roared, thrusting his head into the headrest. No sooner did Henry distance himself from the pack than he slammed on the brakes. The speedometer retreated from 160 to 20 miles per hour. He was stopped cold in traffic.

Henry's followers hastened to take the bait. He accelerated and then slowed amidst gaps in traffic. His cavalcade continued their pursuit, following each of his maneuvers; never letting him get too far out in front. Henry pressed a button on his steering wheel, calling Harmony's cell phone.

"Surprise, surprise, if I don't have the honor of speaking to the man himself. To what do I owe the pleasure Henry?"

"No time for small talk, Harmony. Bring your partner Hoffman and make your way to the Golden Gate Bridge, ASAP. You'll know what I'm talking about when you get there." Click.

Henry turned onto the Bay Bridge. The sky was clear, until he looked towards the City. San Francisco looked as if it had been swallowed by a cloud. He moved to within five feet of the car in front of him and then slowed to fifty miles per hour. Keep them close through the fog.

Henry exited Interstate 80 to U.S. Route 101, towards the tips of the now visible red spires of the fogged in Golden Gate. So many motionless nights staring at the spans, the cables . . . every last detail of that bridge. Within minutes, the bridge would now decide his fate.

Henry entered the bridge on the San Francisco side, heading towards Marin. He slowed the Audi and began weaving between lanes. Frustrated vehicles honked their horns as he slowed all northbound traffic. Then, at a larger gap, he spun the Audi horizontally across both of the easternmost lanes. All northbound traffic came to a standstill. Southbound traffic slowed as passersby paused to see the cause of the commotion.

He stepped out in the middle of the bridge, just where the suspension lines dipped. Nothing obstructed the views to the east and west. Henry snatched a backpack out of the passenger seat, hopped over the rail onto the pedestrian walkway on the east side of the bridge, and began to scramble up onto the cable itself.

Behind him traffic piled up as other passengers started to gather around him.

The forty-mile-an-hour winds caused the entire bridge to sway slightly. He stumbled crossing the cable walkway but held himself steady at the bridge's outer railing.

A woman pointed at him. "We have a jumper!"

"Give him space," someone yelled.

"Don't do it!"

"Life gets better."

The crowd grew larger. They began to close in on him.

Henry picked out some of the faces in the crowd. Melvin Entz, Lewis Chase, Gerald Burke, and a spattering of other clients – titans of their industries. His competitors, Hoffman and Winter. The hired help – Jack Buston, Agent Terry, Agent Parker and the two thugs. They all stood there, waiting, watching.

He scanned their faces. Hundreds of people were now looking at him, fearful for his safety, hungry for the excitement. He was the center of attention.

Showtime.

"I guess you didn't expect this, did you?" he yelled. "But then again, this makes your jobs much easier, doesn't it? Why get your hands messy, when I can do the dirty work myself? Sound familiar? Do you suppose distancing yourself from the dirt keeps your hands clean? We're all guilty!"

Henry secured his backpack, swung his legs over the outer railing and hung on with one hand. Nothing now separated him from the sea below.

The bridge was now a parking lot. Law enforcement began to break through the crowd, moving toward him.

"Take out your cell phone cameras," Henry said.

The wind carried away his command.

"Take out your cameras," he shouted. "Or I will jump."

People looked down, most of them anyway.

"Don't pretend to be ashamed! We're a culture of opportunists, eager to make our mark through YouTube or the evening news. Why should it make you uncomfortable to actually see the face of your victim? Take out your cameras!"

"He said take out your cameras people," a lady yelled, "now!"

One by one cell phones appeared.

"Now record!" Henry said. "Believe me, you won't want to miss this."

The spectators began to record Henry.

Law enforcement officers had him surrounded and they now began to close in on him. When one of them came within five feet, Henry unzipped his backpack and reached in.

"He has something in his hand!" the officer yelled.

"Stand down officer!" The Chief of Police shouted.

In one, swift motion, Henry emptied the contents of his backpack into the ocean below. The material disappeared from view until the wind caught it and blew it east. The gusts caused the matter to unfurl and assemble.

"It looks like a flag," somebody shouted.

"It says something on it."

A banner with large letters appeared behind Henry. The crowd strained to make out the message as the wind beat the canvas. The cords holding the banner unraveled and tightened. In an instant the print became legible. The crowd gasped at the spectacle.

HENRYMADDOX.COM.

Then a massive gust of wind blew Henry off of the bridge.

The crowd sprinted to the edge of the bridge. No trace of Henry. Only fog.

"Wow. That was insane!" A young man on a bike said. "He was right. I was glad I got that recorded." He stuffed his phone into a saddle bag and rode towards the city.

*Before entering
upon so grave a matter
as the destruction
of our national fabric,
with all its benefits,
its memories,
and its hopes,
would it not be wise
to ascertain precisely
why we do it?*

- Abraham Lincoln,
"First Inaugural Address,"
Monday, March 4, 1861

CHAPTER 36

"Laroy, you're going to want to see this." Margaret said.

She was watching a cooking show while in the kitchen when her program was interrupted by a special news report. Laroy left his home office to join her in the kitchen.

"We just received this video footage from a firsthand source at the Golden Gate Bridge," the news reporter said.

The video showed a henrymaddox.com banner unfurl as a man disappeared into the fog.

"This video shows Henry Maddox, the marketing provocateur turn profamily advocate in a promotional performance that appears to have gone terribly wrong. Our onsite reporter, Gretchen Wong has reactions from eyewitnesses, Gretchen."

"Yes Tina, in what appeared to be a publicity stunt, Henry Maddox stopped traffic on the Golden Gate Bridge and then went to the edge of the bridge to unfurl a henrymaddox.com banner. The high winds then pulled Dr. Maddox off of the bridge. George Martinez was on the bridge when it happened. Mr. Martinez, what happened?"

"I was traveling across the bridge to work this morning when traffic stalled to a crawl. Everyone was out of their cars and surrounding some guy. I shut off my car and ran over to see what was going on. This guy was on the outside of the railing asking everyone to take out their cell phone video cameras. At first, nobody wanted to do it, but then he said he'd jump if they didn't. So everybody started filming the guy. He dumped something out of his backpack. When the wind caught it you could see it was this big banner that said 'henrymaddox.com' on it. But then the wind caught it, and he got pulled off the bridge. The wind was blowing pretty hard. Nobody saw where the guy landed or if he was still alive."

"Thank you George. I now have an officer from the California Highway Patrol with me. Officer Erickson, you have some insight as to Dr. Maddox's chances of survival."

"Well yes Gretchen. Unfortunately, the chances of Dr. Maddox's survival are not very good. Even if he did survive impact, once he hit the water, he would suffer hypothermia.

He wouldn't be able to last long in these cold ocean temperatures."

"Thank you officer. And there you have it, Dr. Henry Maddox appears to be lost at sea. We'll let you know more as we receive more information. Reporting live from San Francisco Five News, I'm Gretchen Wong."

Laroy shutoff the television and stared at the blank screen. He couldn't believe it. And, actually, the more he thought about it, the more he realized he literally couldn't believe it.

"Henry was too smart to die in some cockamamie stunt, Margaret," he said.

"Whatever happened Laroy, you know media outlets are going to be coming to you with questions. You better decide what the next henrymaddox.com campaign is going to be. Henry wouldn't want you to waste this publicity."

L aroy clicked publish from his computer. Over fifteen million subscribers received the following message:

> When I first met Henry Maddox, he was a man motivated by profit at the expense of community. Today he has mobilized millions through his henrymaddox.com campaigns; a virtual community intent on empowering the exploited.
>
> A little of Henry Maddox exists in each of us. We scratch and claw for financial gain and then in

our quiet, sober moments we wonder about our legacy. Do our efforts produce a genuine benefit? Or do we simply profit at the expense of others? Do we pillage or do we build? Do we yield to what Abraham Lincoln called our "better angels of our nature?"

Greed has reached every corner of our culture. It now threatens our entire way of life. This thing we call an economy has little to do with increasing our productive capacity. We have confused progress with financial gain. It will take cooperation to identify, confront, expose, and reverse these tendencies. Will you be one of the courageous souls who band with us in our cause?

As was the case for Henry Maddox, so it is with you. It's never too late to change.

DO YOUR PART: Watch for our call to action. The henrymaddox.com cause has just begun.

"Destruction is not profit."
– Frederic Bastiat (1850)

"People are not products."
– Henry Maddox (2013)

———

Cargo vessels moved at reduced speeds as they passed under the Golden Gate Bridge. With their vision obscured by the fog, safety and news helicopters retreated from the area around the bridge. Within an hour, dive teams were dispatched in search of Henry's body. They searched under the bridge and further out into the bay. The tide was going out when he jumped.

At about the same time, a sea plane following a GPS transmitter signal, landed a mile or so upstream from the bridge.

The pilot coasted to a standstill almost on top of the coordinates. A minute later, a man pulled himself up onto the pontoon.

The pilot opened his door. "You all right? Water's frigid."

"It's all right," Henry said. "I've got a wet suit on. Have any trouble finding me in the fog?"

"Nah. I've been flying by instruments for years. Though this is about the craziest job I've ever taken. How about you? Any trouble getting down?"

"No. I've been base jumping off of bridges for years."

The pilot noticed that the parachute, loosely spread in the water, had writing on it. "Got your luggage in the back and some hot food. Figure you must have worked up an appetite."

"Thanks. That was good of you. That reminds me, did you bring that weight?"

The pilot fished under his seat, where he'd secured a ten pound barbell weight, and handed it to Henry. Henry slipped out of his parachute harness, clipped the weight to it, and dropped it into the bay. The parachute flared for a moment, letting the pilot read it before it disappeared beneath the water. Henrymaddox.com.

Henry stood on the pontoon, clinging to a strut, then clambered into the cockpit. "You can change into some dry clothes before we take off," the pilot said. "That will make you feel better."

"If it's all the same to you, I'd prefer to get going. This place will be crawling with Coast Guard in a couple of minutes."

"Whatever you say. You're the boss."

Henry reached in his pack and pulled out a stack of hundred dollar bills wrapped in waterproof bags. "Here's the rest of what I owe you. Half for taking the job and the other half for doing it. Thank you. You're a man of your word."

"I'm a man who needs the money. Now buckle up, we have some miles ahead of us."

The engine roared to life, and the plane took off to the north through the fog.

*. . . I have sworn
on the altar of God,
eternal hostility
against every form of tyranny
over the mind of man.*

- Thomas Jefferson
Letter to Dr. Benjamin Rush
September 23, 1800

EPILOGUE

One Week Later

Pressley swung open the door to the henrymaddox.com office. Thomas trailed close behind. "Cheryl, you'll never guess what I just got."

"Whatever it was, it must be pretty awesome. I haven't seen you this happy in a long time."

Pressley held up an envelope.

"What's that?"

"It's my student loan statement."

"And you're happy you received it?"

"Uh, yeah. It says my balance is zero."

"Really? Did they make a mistake?"

"No, I called on it and they said that somebody paid it off, in full."

"You're one lucky girl. Who would have done something like that?"

"Unless I have a rich uncle I don't know about, it could only have been one of two people. So, was it you or Laroy?"

"Although I love you like a sister Pressley, I can tell you for sure it wasn't me. I've been too busy taking care of all of Henry's property to worry about doing something that thoughtful for someone else."

"That's right, Professor Maddox signed all his property over to you prior to . . ."

"Yeah . . . the incident."

Pressley and Cheryl paused, their faces sober.

"How's the property management going?" Thomas asked.

"It's keeping me busy. I'm selling the San Francisco home. I couldn't stand to live there alone. Everything in that place reminds me of Henry. I may keep the Tahoe cabin. I still don't feel comfortable driving around in that race car of his, though. Everybody eyeballs me when I drive that thing. I really don't like that sort of attention."

"Is Laroy coming in today?" Pressley asked.

"Yeah he should be in here any minute."

"Cheryl."

"Yes Pressley."

"Do you think Henry is still alive?"

"I honestly don't know," Cheryl said. "I like to think he is."

"Do you think we'll ever know?" Pressley asked.

"I hope so," Cheryl said.

"Regardless of whether he's alive or not, he will always live on in our memories," a new voice said.

"Oh, hello, Laroy. I didn't see you come in."

"I snuck in the back."

"Thank you Laroy!" Pressley threw her arms around Laroy.

"Why the affection?" Laroy asked. "Not that I'm complaining, mind you."

"For paying off my student loan, of course," Pressley said.

"Ah. Except that I didn't pay your student loan off Pressley. I'm sorry."

"Well if you didn't then who did?" Pressley said.

"Maybe it's a mistake," Thomas said.

"Wow, that's weird," Cheryl said looking at her iPhone.

"What?" Pressley said.

"I just got a tweet from henrymaddox.com," Cheryl said. "I thought only Laroy and I knew the password to tweet from that account. Do you think we were hacked?"

"What did the tweet say?" Laroy asked.

HENRY MADDOX LIVES . . .

Continue the conversation at henrymaddox.com . . .

ABOUT THE AUTHOR

Patrick Ord grew up in San Diego, CA as one of five boys. He attended Brigham Young University, ultimately earning both a Bachelor and Master's degree in Accounting with an emphasis in Information Systems. At nineteen, Patrick interrupted his studies at Brigham Young to serve a two year Spanish speaking Mission for his church in New York City: serving in the Spanish speaking areas of Brooklyn, The Bronx, Queens, and Manhattan. After returning from his mission, Patrick met his wife Emily at BYU. Patrick and Emily currently have four children and reside in Utah.

After obtaining his degrees, Patrick worked in the high tech industry in both Orange County and the Bay Area of California. He has also worked in the home building and real estate development industry; participating in projects throughout the Southwest. Patrick currently owns his own management consulting company.

The Curtain is Patrick Ord's first novel.

Made in the USA
Middletown, DE
09 November 2014